# LIVING
# YOUR LIFE
## A Humanist Guide
## to Well Being

Lynda W. Schmidt LCSW
Jungian Psychoanalyst

Klaus D. Schmidt   PhD

authorHOUSE™

*1663 LIBERTY DRIVE, SUITE 200*
*BLOOMINGTON, INDIANA 47403*
*(800) 839-8640*
*WWW.AUTHORHOUSE.COM*

*First published by AuthorHouse 06/29/05*


*ISBN: 1-4208-5494-1 (sc)*


*Library of Congress Control Number: 2005904017*
*Printed in the United States of America*

*Bloomington, Indiana*
*This book is printed on acid-free paper.*

*Bildarchiv Preussischer Kulturbesitz / Art Resource, NY.*

# *Dedication*

THE UNEXAMINED LIFE IS NOT
WORTH LIVING
Socrates

This book is dedicated to our parents,
who gave all they could.

# Contents

# Introduction:

Well over 2000 years ago Socrates suggested that a full life, a complete life, a rich life is based on analyzing one's existence. He does not, however, lend his insight as to whether this task should be accomplished via introspection, or with the help of others. But we have the timeless saying that " a joy shared is twice the joy and a trouble shared is half the trouble". This advice precedes Freud who is given credit for recognizing that "talking things out" resolves psychological problems. Today, neurological research confirms Freud's intuition.

Western societies are currently flooded with a vast array of possible solutions to our nearly universal modern day "Angst". We use this term intentionally to describe what many, if not most of us, perceive to be the very absence of a rich, full life.

It is our intent to combine a number of psychological realties with a dose of philosophy, even some speculative proposals, all aimed at successful self analysis and ultimately a deeper sense of life, making our trip on earth more satisfying.

What we will offer might be viewed as a mirror, but a mirror which talks back. A journey, together, going back to our first memories, and slowly reviewing impact filled events, memorable emotions, and digging up happenings deeply buried by us in our minds in order to make them less painful.

Is life little more than an effort to maximize pleasure while minimizing pain? We see this approach as zero sum game, a surrender to little more than just "getting by". It is our objective to reach a new level of true satisfaction about life with ourselves and others.

From our first day on earth on, we are exposed to others. These others often are to a considerable extent responsible for shaping our own lives. This external conditioning we may perceive as positive or negative. We, in turn may find ourselves in a position of influencing the lives of others. The outcomes of these interactions are powerful, putting in question the very concepts of "free will" and self determination.

To begin our trip it is logical to start at the beginning, our childhood, our life with or as parents.

# Chapter 1

# Parents and Children

Nature has imbued many of its species with what are best called instincts. These are inbred, automatic actions and reactions. In most mammals motherhood includes many vital survival systems. They include feeding offspring and providing security and protection. As the young grow, they are given lessons preparing them for adult life. Lion cubs are taught to hunt and little birds are edged to the side of the nest, tempting them to fly. Even social life lessons may be included in the curriculum. Animals which live in groups, like monkeys and elephants, prepare the young who must adapt to communal life manners and behavior.

In many species the male, the father, participates in the child rearing process. As far as our mammalian relatives are concerned the father contribution is sketchy. Communal animals seem to involve the males more with roles focusing on security and communal life lessons.

For many species, however, the male's role ends with copulation and bringing up the kids is left to mom.

Why is it then that when it comes to humankind we are faced with daily reminders that one or several aspects of basic child rearing have been violated? Children are abused in a variety of ways, left to fend for themselves, physically and psychologically abandoned, then propped in front of the TV to provide them with life lessons. All too often mothers alone are saddled with the rearing task, men having done their job with fertilization, or being too busy with their work lives to contribute and share the responsibility.

If we credit instincts to the animal world, human beings have introduced the mysterious concept of LOVE to the equation. We casually sign off letters with "love". We love a favorite vacation spot, a certain actor or a television program. We love working with specific fellow employees and limit the concept to only certain extended family members. What this array exposes is that we use "love" as an amorphous concept to try and validate our own sense of approval and disapproval of a multitude of life issues with this word.

Love in human terms almost defies definition. It is more than acceptance, it is near unconditional approval. Love overcomes temporary rejection, is permanent. Love means mutual support, aid and comfort. It is maintained via ongoing reassurance. It is tangible and intangible. If these conditions sound lofty and beyond accomplishment, it is no wonder that we seek confirmation in religion. God's love only, in Christian terminology, seems to fulfill what real love calls for. This also implies that we seem to sense that our human relationships do not offer what is needed to fill our own personal love cups.

As parents we are supposed to love our children. Do we in fact do so? Regrettably not always, if we try to live by the standards outlined above. This observation is not limited to our teen-agers who tend to be deeply, but rightly objectionable. Babies may be an unwanted result of a brief relationship, or the outcome of carelessness. Children may not turn out to be what we wanted them to be. They are a nuisance, a burden, a costly item demanding time and effort, often without any perceivable payback or gratitude.

Consistent violence and physical or sexual abuse are obvious and flagrant issues leading to troubled minds. We have been amazed that such excesses are frequently repressed by the victims. This is an unconscious activity which takes place automatically, filing the experienced terror in low levels of the psyche. They are not forgotten, but left to fester and disturb the afflicted. Often this situation leads to psychosomatic illnesses. This involves the body paying the price for the repressed brew which has been left unearthed, in order to avoid the pain of re-living horrifying experiences.

If you have suffered from such abuse we advise that you seek professional help. Your troubles defy home repair. But it is up to you to be willing to dig up and explore your experiences. This is likely to become a very painful process requiring outside support. Like much psychological healing, and this central point will be repeated again and again, YOU must be willing and interested to get help. YOU must take the initiative.

There is ample clinical evidence that mother and embryo are more than two separate units connected via a food pipeline. Much publicity has been given to abstinence from alcohol and smoking by pregnant women. Now we know that mother and embryo form a symbiotic unit, a one. Drugs are shared and even the body proteins generated by the brain in emotional experiences are shared. All of this inflow may leave a permanent mark on the evolving human. These may be permanent blemishes which may be hard if not impossible to repair.

We know of a multitude of examples based on pre-birth exposure. One case was a man with a great number of allergic reactions. It was soon discovered that his mother, suffering from frequent migraines, sought relief in large doses of aspirin. Aspirin turned out to be the first and prominent allergy in his case. As time passed he proved to be allergic to an ever increasing number of medications.

Another example was a deeply anxious young woman whose prevalent memory of her mother was her anxiousness. Even though the daughter left home at an early age, trying to separate herself from an uncongenial parental home, her inbred anxiety persisted. It is our opinion that perceived damage dating to the early time in life calls less for analytical work, but support and re-assurance from those we cherish around us.

After birth, the mother-baby relationship is primary. This interaction is critical and involves far more than feeding and basic comfort. The infant who is appreciated, approved of and made to feel secure has been given the seeds of self esteem. This sense of self approval validates all of us in later years. This tangible issue is supplemented by a trio of intangibles. The approval given a baby tends to foster the development of faith, trust and hope. The existence of these three irrational concepts in human beings gives rise to the reaction of " I am ok" and "it is going to be ok."

The mother-child relationship is not one sided. Babies learn quickly how to attract the attention of their support system. They cry if they do not feel well and scream when hungry or anxious. Ideally a mutual system is created wherein the sensitive mother builds a relationship which fulfills the child's expectations. A failure to establish this linkage and support is likely to result in an anxious and insecure child. These two double negatives subsequently carry over into adulthood.

Fred, who suffered from occasional anxiety, spoke ill of his parents. Their relationship tenuous and both of them were insecure and anxious. His mother was deeply depressed much of the time. Yet, he found comfort with his grandmother who stood by him and comforted him when needed. This is an indication that troublesome parental care may be supplied instead by others whom the child trusts.

A common complaint about parents involves the perception that either one of them, or even both "did not like me". We advisedly use the term perception. This means that we felt disliked even though the parent may have had no or few negative feelings about us. You may have been scolded for being "too touchy". Too touchy is a misinterpretation. If you are "touchy", there is a reason and a cause for you being so. As a result you are more sensitive to criticism and all else that comes across as a negative expression or feeling directed at you.

The issue of sensitivity lends itself to self-discovery and can be ameliorated via reality checking. If and when you feel offended, as soon as possible as you realize the resulting feelings, STOP and THINK about what happened. Separate your feelings and try to set them aside allowing you to engage in what is called a cognitive appraisal of the event. Thinking can ease painful feelings. Thinking can be used as a balance, even as an offset to feelings. Be as specific as you can be. What words caused your feelings of being hurt and offended? Was the intent to hurt, or was it perhaps to correct something objectionable to the other party. Did you possibly react very strongly, in a way others may view as over-react? This, a very common turn in the sensitive personality. Again, your reaction is YOU and real to you. There is a reason for your reaction, a cause which may date to your past, triggered by the present event. Can you devalue the happening from painful, to "no big deal"? When you think about the event again, perhaps it was in fact a minor issue, best put to rest.

Your cognitive evaluation may call for a response. You may feel that too much has been invested in the issue and that in order to set it straight, you need to react. Once again it would be wise to push your feelings, which may indeed be strong, onto a side track. This despite the fact that your feelings were and are you and are true. If a discussion of the event is necessary, it is entirely appropriate for you to express your feelings about what took place. But the solution of the conflict should be sought on tangible issues, the facts of the case, so to speak. Address them with an eye to lowering the intensity of the debate and focusing on proposals aimed at solving the problem. Seek a compromise satisfactory to both, meaning a win-win outcome. Indeed there may be no satisfying solution to the conflict. Then you must call on your internal strength, mature feeling and conscious evaluation to tolerate a disagreement.

Two dominant and common complaints about parental relationships relate to the extremes of the child parent interaction. Either too much control, or too little. The former tends to result in rebelliousness, the latter in a sense of abandonment and a perceived lack of being loved. Both issues require a deeper look with a call to you to check into your memories and to single out those which have left an impact. In fact you may discover that both, too much parental control and perceived neglect pop up concurrently.

It has been well established that patterns set in childhood and in infancy persist through a life span. We have pointed at the critical relationship between mother and child. Men, in recent history were seen as the bread winners, and their role in the family tended to focus on authority. Modern social values have brought a dramatic change to the "traditional" role of the father. This is particularly true in the United Sates. Indeed accepting and submitting to authority is still a lesson to be learned from the father. For a son, his father is a guide to masculinity. Other tasks of modern man were seen as more feminine in the past. Fathers should be supportive, and yes, loving. This includes validating, supporting and comforting the offspring. Enforcing the law of the house, so to speak, does not preclude offering approval when warranted. Both parents must assure and re-assure their children in their search for a safe path through life.

All too often we have heard that children, especially sons, were little more than a clone, an extension of dad. Offspring was expected to make up for the disappointments of one or the other parent. Unrelenting pressure was put on children to perform or outperform a parent, live up to ever higher standards, impossible to achieve. Parental expectations all too often lead to disappointment and a loss of self esteem in children.

Typical reactions to an unsatisfying youth include passivity and defeatism, aggression and hostility and insecurity with anxiety. As children, we have little control, nor the reasoning or intellect to evaluate our experiences. As adults, however, we not only have the capacity to remember, but also to re-think what happened to us. Here our self mirroring process can be very constructive. It may be useful for you to write down all events which come to mind, events which left a mark. Then, try and experience your feelings as you had them and validate or change them from your adult perspective. Then think about the experience as objectively as you can. Lastly never fail to talk such issues over with those you trust.

To conclude, it is our objective to treat negative childhood memories like dirty laundry. It needs to be pulled out of the laundry bin, examined and washed. Our objective is to have stains and dirt washed out and sent down the drain, leaving you with a clean psychic wardrobe.

## Chapter 2

# Mind and Body

We must begin with a compelling and absolute statement. Mind and body are ONE. This fact is not limited to what is called the autonomous interaction of brain and body. We take it for granted that the complex automatic operations of our glands, our digestion, our heartbeat and our breathing , just to mention a few, are managed by our brain. What has now become a reality is that our emotions also affect our body. A contemporary example is that stress causes symptoms. The body reacts with high blood pressure, painful muscle spasms and a multitude of other physical malfunctions. The word psychosomatic (mind-body) has become an everyday expression in our health analyses. You, in your own experience may have felt physically and mentally better after your physician gave you comfort, reassurance and support, more than a rational diagnosis.

Many of the top medical schools now include in their programs courses on basic psychology with an eye to personal and emotional interaction between patient and doctor. But still, all too many physicians tend to view their patients as pure biological structure. This is akin to a car being tended to by a mechanic, leaving out the driver. It takes both of them to operate the vehicle. And to operate the vehicle successfully, both must be in good condition working together harmoniously.

Our psyche (Greek for soul) might be viewed as a multi story structure. The top floors are occupied with what is happening now and governed by the ego. (Latin for I) This concept is our perception of who and what we are. As we descend into the deeper levels of our minds we ultimately reach the "unconscious". This is a storeroom for what Jung called "archetypes", images passed on to us from generation to generation. In it are also impressions and memories gathered from our species' earliest days on earth forward. Add to this repressed emotions, feelings about events which at the time they were perceived were too difficult or painful to integrate into our conscious and accessible memory. Some have compared the unconscious with a kettle in which we cook our own witches brew.

It has been suggested that if the essential mother-child bonding in its earliest stage is perceived as wanting or lacking by the baby, the infant may generate a permanent rage firmly planted in the unconscious. (Kohut). This rage keeps boiling within us and rather than gaining the light of day consciously, expresses itself via a multitude of psychosomatic illnesses.

We propose that it is more than rage that cooks down below. Deep sadness experienced and too painful to bear at the time, will be submerged in the brew. Powerfully frightening occurrences may be shuttled away to put them out of reach, leaving fear as a potent component of our inner being.

Filing events and emotions into our less accessible memory banks may be an intentional effort. Suppressing unpleasant events and feelings is something we all do on the premise that "we cannot bear to think about them". The accumulation of this mass provides another sizeable fermenting and disturbing component of our psychic septic tank. On the positive side, suppressed emotions remain accessible and we can make conscious efforts to dig them up, relive them and try to defuse them. Time having passed will give us new and better perspectives to reevaluate these emotions and give us the opportunity to file them away without pain.

It should also be recognized that the unconscious is not only a storage place for painful and scary experiences, but is also the locus where our creativity and development originate. So, as we plumb the depths to clear ourselves of trouble, we also activate exciting new possibilities.

What emerges from these observations is the likelihood that our psyche is highly stimulated to seek expression through our body if we offer no relief via consciously opening a relief valve. The result is the current epidemic of psychosomatic sickness. Day in day out stress, childhood events and our unconscious stew, all crying for discovery, but too painful for us to accomplish. Consequently we pay with physical pain. Psychosomatic illnesses are NOT imaginary, phony stuff, something "all in your head". They are REAL. Do they require medical attention? For your peace of mind and to make certain that you do not suffer from a treatable physical disorder, a checkup is a good idea.

Now, however, we reach a critical junction. Most physicians will seek to identify your problem through traditional diagnoses. This means finding a physical reason for the malfunction. You may be subjected to a series of tests, often ending in "inconclusive" results. Your body is complaining, but NOT doing any identifiable harm. This is an alarm for YOU to heed. A warning that mind work needs to be done. Your witches' brew is boiling over.

Psychosomatic illnesses tend to follow fashion. Admitting that we have mental trouble is still frequently viewed as "abnormal" and is a social stigma. Three, four generations ago it was headaches and migraines which were an approved way of showing distress. Going back 30 to 50 years, stomach ulcers were fashionable. Today, PAIN is current. Back pain, tendonitis, muscles, joints, and of course, migraines are still with us. The trendiest pain and muscle spasm is the frozen shoulder syndrome. Auto immune disorders and allergies are the rage; asthma, mysterious fibromyalgia, urinary tract infections, chronic fatigue syndrome are an endless list of misery where the origins remain clouded. But if you are on to yourself, YOU have the opportunity to call the bluff, to call the hand your mind is holding.

You are not alone. Carl provides a stunning case history. His unresolved inner turmoil resulted in this impressive list of illnesses. Most of them got medical attention, some improved through medication, some resulted in surgery. At one time or other, sometimes concurrently, he suffered from:

Hives
Skin eruptions
Back muscle pain, spasms
Nerve pain
Tendon pain
Long term leg muscle pain
Bladder spasms
Liver malfunction
Constipation
Intestinal cramps
Irregular heartbeat
Dizziness
Periodic loss of taste
Gout
Nasal congestion
Allergies
Local oral infections
Eye lid infections.
Prostatitis

A first glance one might be tempted to consider hypochondria, perhaps a prime example of a "basket case". In fact Carl was a successful executive and functioned in all aspects of life. But he was in pain, both mentally and physically. When he recognized that once one symptom had improved, only to be replaced by another one, he sought analytical help. His steady improvement is more than a case history, but offers a formula for a cure.

We offered a two pronged approach. The first involved an unearthing of deep seated childhood problems. As an infant he experienced what he felt was a loss of love. In later years his father appeared to reject him. As an adult, his feelings of diminishment and rejection let painful memories reappear.

Clearly an important process took place. Carl began to focus on his mind, on his painful emotions, LESS on his body reactions. As time passed he was able to self diagnose ongoing physical disturbances as somatic reactions to his ongoing discovery of psychic pain. Even better, frequently when a symptom made an appearance, he was able to banish it, affecting a self cure by referring it to his mind.

It is our view that painful emotions, most likely suppressed many years ago, are the cause of the contemporary epidemic of pain. It is up to you to let these emotions see the light of day and gain RECOGNITION. Feeling, experiencing the pain will bring you relief.

You may find that your body complaints are so loud and dominant that you cannot access your cooler, insightful self. This is a good time to practice a basic relaxation procedure: deep breathing. First take time to find a comfortable space where you can either lie down or sit at ease. Then breathe in, DEEPLY, with your belly literally sticking out, hold your breath for a moment, then exhale, again deeply, to the bottom of your lungs. When inhaling think of the clean air reaching you, and when exhaling propel all that is bothering you to the outside. Do this slowly and deliberately for five minutes and feel yourself relax.

Our society has become focused on pain avoidance through medication. Pain is trying to tell you something. Might this be physical or mental pain. Painting it over with pills will give you temporary relief, but will not provide a cure.

Modern pharmacology has provided us with a multitude of medications designed to offer relief from depression, stress, anxiety and other painful psychic malfunctions. We are not against the use these ameliorants. In a time of crisis they can rebalance you so that you can work on the true source of your problems.

We implied that the range of psychosomatic illnesses is vast, far greater than the medical community wants to acknowledge. Admittedly some of the following material is speculative, but is based on the experience in our practice and a multitude of case histories. What may affect our health may be a combination of genes, inherited vulnerability, viruses and bacteria and chemicals absorbed from the outside. Finally all of these components are massaged by our minds. This mental component can have both positive or negative influence on our health.

A positive outlook on our fate, a degree of lightheartedness can help us overcome illness. A famous case well illustrated by Norman Cousins involved the application of "positive emotions" and humor to help him overcome a serious case of rheumatoid arthritis. The pessimistic patient, the one who sees health as a continuous threat and on a downward spiral, is likely to lose much of the psychic support needed for healing.

Outside support can be offered from several meaningful sources. Family, friends, spiritual advisers and of course, the physician on the job. Their positive attitude will have a major impact on your recovery, a process we refer to as HEALING. Two studies indicated that prayer for a sick person by a group of outsiders had positive results, even when the patient was unaware of the prayers.

Our experience with some contemporary widespread health problems provided some general observations. High blood pressure, often blamed on "stress" had in fact deeper psychic roots. We found that contained, suppressed deep emotions were at the bottom of this dangerous problem. In case after case we noticed patients living their lives the way they were supposed to live them, as opposed to the lives they wanted to live. Frustration and deep inner disappointment resulted in the potentially life threatening physical reaction.

Medication has been successfully used to address this situation. In our view this may help with the symptom, but not with its cause. One of the more difficult questions for most people is "what do you want from life, or how would you like to live?" The dilemma of what we seek and can reasonably accomplish is perplexing for many of us. Finding the answer and attempting to live it out is step one to ameliorating several difficulties, including high blood pressure. All this involves internal discovery, reality checking and the development of workable outcomes. Completion of all these steps is well within your own competence. Ideal solutions can not always be reached. We found that simple exercise done on a regular basis alleviates this health problem for some people. Others improved through the pursuit of hobbies, fulfilling a mini passion so to speak. Creativity may also provide relief.

It may appear a stretch too far to suggest that cancer has a psychic connection. But we found that some patients could be helped via psychological discovery. Two attitudes stood out in the cases we treated. One, that life was not worth living. A deep sense of disappointment needed to be flushed out and its cause to be aired. The second displayed an attitude of "being good, doing good". The suppression of "bad" thoughts and the denial of personal darkness appeared to be a possible cause for cancer. These patients suffered through their great pain with smiles and goodwill. Here we succeeded by introducing the negative, sometimes called the shadow side of the victim. For them this involved overcoming self criticism, their minds unwilling to see the negative in themselves. When this reality, which is a part of all of us, was accepted and integrated by the patient, healing was possible.

Heart disease, a "broken heart" is another contemporary health problem under attack through a variety of approaches. Diet and exercise are the highlights of the preventative campaign. We found repetitive psychological patterns in our practice. Our cases tended to be angry, even full of rage and expressed great hostility at the slightest provocation. They were aggressive "go-getters". Without exception our patients, after considerable psychological work, found a loss of love at the root of their illness. This loss of love included abandonment, rejection or death of a loved one with time frames going back to infancy and forward to current events. Our work included close cooperation with the physicians on the case, and with our dual approach of healing psychic wounds and repairing damaged hearts, we saw improvement.

Our society is submerged in addictions. Even just a partial listing indicates an epidemic. Drugs, both legal and illegal; alcohol in its many forms, food, good or bad, but lots of it. Add tobacco, and sex, now aided with ED pharmaceuticals, beginning with young people and still attempted with dogged determination in senior circles. Work and drinking often combine in the workaholic. Another well known addiction is compulsive shopping.

An escape from something, sometimes is an escape to something, like feelings of peace and satisfaction. What are we running away from? When searching for clues with our cases, we found that psychic pain is the culprit. Anxiety, fear and unexpressed sorrow were drowned in an addiction. Easing the pain the objective.

This objective is not an exclusive symptom of western societies, but a global phenomenon. The underlying cause is basic: life is hard. However what is novel to contemporary society is that we have the pain killers, not only to dull the pain over the long term, but also to damage ourselves permanently through the overuse of addictive substances and activities.

Uncovering and exposing the sources of pain may call for professional help, especially if the damage was caused many years ago. More recent events can be dealt with cognitively by you. Again a confidant may be an able sounding board. Sharing your true feelings with another will ease the pain, and discussing your perception of the facts may shed more light, and insight from another perspective on your problem.

This list could be expanded to book form. Your mind and your body are in constant communication. The results of this interaction are not only body symptoms but real illness. To be well and stay well, you must care for both: BODY and MIND.

# Chapter 3

# Going with the Flow

Who are you really? Carl Jung has come to the rescue by offering to dissect us by what he calls "personality types." If and when you are able to figure out what makes you tick, you not only will find it easier to live with yourself, but also with others. Going counter to who you are creates barriers, can even make you sick.

Your personality is the sum of your attitudes, perceptions and judgments. These components lay the ground for your behavior, your relatedness and interaction, and the way you adapt to life.

It has been debated at length as to who and what made you the way you are, and when this formula setting occurs. Further, is this YOU a fixed identity, or can, or will you change over time? No doubt you have been in despair at times over your inability to cope or adapt to difficult and changing situations. Take heart. Not only do we change, but we can learn to fill in areas of our personality where we seem to be underdeveloped. Even more importantly, whichever personality traits describe you, not only are they the very YOU, but they are normal. There is nothing pathological about you even if it feels at times that you are out of synch with others, or maybe even with yourself.

No doubt we are delivered on earth with a basic predisposition, a basic prefabricated personality. This original setup is changed by our environment with our family being the first change agent. The social bias of the culture within which we live molds us further. To illustrate this point, all we need to do is recognize our collective propensity in the US toward extraversion, casting introverts into the role of the outsider. Even current events reshape our personality. But when all is said and done, change or not, we tend to be identifiable by a set of traits, might they be innate or learned.

We all are familiar with the concept of extraversion. This concept describes a basic attitude with which we approach life. It is the all-American trait. It describes a person who is outgoing, at ease with others, a good mixer. Jokingly extraverts have been accused of wanting to be alone in only one place, the toilet. Normal for them is to be outwardly directed, both toward people and objects. They love worldly things and are comfortable in groups.

Psychologically, extraverts seek out others not only for company, but to validate themselves. Via this mirroring process they get confirmation and gain self esteem. In this process also lies the hidden danger that when approval is lacking, worse should rejection occur, the extravert is more easily injured, lacking an inner confirmation of his value. When confronted with material rising from the unconscious, he can be  discomforted, and troubled.

At work, the extrovert leans into his task full bore. He may well overdo it and pay for his desire to succeed or leave an impression with stress symptoms and other ailments. Neglect of body and soul are common in this type.

We Americans make friends easily, as a matter of fact tend to describe our most superficial acquaintances as "friends". Therefore friendships are made quickly and dissolved with equal equanimity.

On the opposite pole of this scale is the introvert. Just think of Gary Cooper in the film High Noon. A loner facing a difficult task and struggling with the solution within and by himself. Introverts come across as remote, removed and somewhat inaccessible. The words "private, do not enter" seem to stand out on their name tag.

The mental processes and energies of the introvert are inwardly directed.  This self sufficiency results in a quiet, reflective, low profile person. Self understanding and focus draws this person from the object to the subject. The inner processes are key and rule over outer stimuli.

In an extraverted society the introvert may be viewed as inferior, or an underdog  or scapegoat. As a reaction to this perception the introvert may attempt to domineer and may come across as egotistical.

Introverts chose their friends with great care. The resulting relationships are deeper and long lasting. If we accept that Americans as a society are extraverted, the English, the Swiss and the Japanese tend toward the introverted mode. There privacy is respected as a norm for behavior. Social mores are governed by complex rules of behavior and social intercourse. All of them designed to protect the individual.

We can view the extravert-introvert axis as linear, but like a camel's back with two humps. Most people tend to be on either end of this line, though not at the extreme end, nor in the middle. Extreme personalities stick out like sore thumbs and are relatively rare. Jung encourages us to learn about our "inferior" function, meaning the other end of the line. We all harbor both extraversion and introversion within us. Yet one attitude is dominant, and learning about our other side, Jung views as growth.

Another axis Jung proposes has "thinking" on one end and "feeling" on the other. All day long we gather data, and these two functions are used to process this input. Thinking is the application of logic to the data aiming for a solution or result  Feeling is the subjective evaluation of the gathered information, leading to a choice and selection by preference. Thinking targets right or wrong answers, feeling is about best and worst choices.  An example of the thinking approach might be a physicist using  constructs and formulas to manipulate data and solve a problem.

Subtle differences appear between introverted thinking types and extraverted thinkers. The  introvert may have trouble explaining his rationale, which is crystal clear to him, but not necessarily to his audience. He may get mired in his own thinking, overlooking the need to relate and communicate on an interpersonal basis. The extraverted thinking type has the natural ability to get his ideas across. Yet he may lack the cohesiveness required for a total picture. This rounding out of  diverse ideas into completed thoughts comes easier to the introvert who uses his inner resources more completely.

We all have feelings, and for many of us that function helps us chose and decide. Our evaluation may hinge on what we perceive as good or bad, or what we like or dislike. Feeling types befriend others easily, having a natural tendency to connect. They relate and are related. It may be a cultural imperative that many more women appear to be feeling types than men. This observation may be in flux as our culture changes with the trend being toward a more even balance of the feeling function between the sexes.

The feeling type tends to be tentative, perhaps even weak in his thinking shoes. And when criticized for thinking lapses, he may well become emotional with a display of "hurt feelings".

Once more we must note that neither function is superior. Both are valid. What is important is that you should recognize which is your strength. If you react with feeling to a thinking statement, a misunderstanding could easily occur. Recognizing where "we come from" and the base others call home, facilitates communications.

One more spectrum developed by Jung must be explored. It contrasts "intuition" with "sensation". Both concepts relate to perception. How do we gather and interpret data. The intuitive does this by hunches, guesses and inspiration. A sensate, on the other hand, gathers and is able to retain many, often unrelated facts. We all have met them when they appear to be walking encyclopedias. Concrete reality and whatever is practical, is their world. The character of Lieutenant Commander

DATA and Spock before him, in the Star Trek series are prototypical sensates.

It is easy to conclude that people of various and differing types can totally misunderstand each other. Failures to communicate may not be willful exercises of bad intent, but simple expressions of who we are. And the process of discovering our strengths and weaknesses is most easily accomplished by discovering our weaknesses. They often are more blatant than our strengths.

We tend to marry the opposite type to our own, thus seeking completion. Our friends, on the other hand, are more likely to mirror us, being the same type as we are. This issue is still being debated, but provides an opportunity for you to typecast both your friends and mates with the aim of identifying them and you correctly.

One more Jungian concept, though not related to "types" should be mentioned. It is his recognition of what he termed "animus" and "anima". These concepts relate to a masculine component in women (animus) and a feminine part (anima) in all men. Recognizing this universal psychological phenomenon should free all of us from stereotypic inhibitions or prohibitions. As one of our clients noted, it is ok for men to cry. And it is equally ok for women to become CEOs or carpenters.

In addition to improving communication, it is helpful to consider typology when interpreting symptoms, both psychological and physical. For instance, the feeling function may be calling for attention when you have intestinal disturbances. By the same token the thinking function may want to be heard when you find yourself physically tense with aching joints and muscles.

Among psychological symptoms, feeling types may express trouble by becoming hysterical, their feelings running amok. Thinking personalities may become compulsive, rigid and perfectionist when confronting psychological difficulties. Both hysteria and compulsion are reactions to deeply troubling experiences; the former a release of frantic feelings, the latter an attempt to control them.

What we must repeat is that we are not one or the other type. We are blends of all of them with most of us featuring dominant traits, what we referred to as a camel's hump. It may be helpful to list a few examples of how we identified some famous Americans.

Perhaps like us, you too are a fan of the Frasier Crane TV series. As we see them, Frasier is an extraverted, feeling, sensation type. His brother Niles, on the other hand, is an introvert with thinking and intuition his other dominant functions. They complement each other, thus as the show illustrates, enjoy spending time together. Former President Clinton has strong and evident features with extraversion, feeling and intuition. Oprah Winfrey demonstrates identical traits. The current President Bush is based on extraversion, thinking and sensation, the same features his mother Barbara carries.

# Chapter 4

# Communicating

ALL communications are purposeful. And if we understand them, meaningful. We may exchange information, each stating a point of view. But this is not communicating which calls for a willingness to accept each other and each other's reality and issue.

To begin with, this vast concept needs to be internalized. Dreaming represents internal conversation. Often dreams are cooked up by our unconscious. This, the deepest level of our psyche is a storeroom of all our experiences, and collective impressions passed on from generation to generation. The latter includes archetypes, and instincts. Archetypes are images imprinted in our minds. such as the father, the clown, the hero, a dragon, an initiation. Our steadily growing conscious mind tends to push these inherited sources ever farther from discovery. But our unconscious can be explored. Dreams draw their messages from our entire psyche, including the unconscious.

Roger had vivid recall of nightmares experienced in his infancy. These recurring dreams had him facing, then falling into infinity, a concept way beyond his understanding. An endless, timeless tumbling frightened him night after night. What was needed at the time was parental reassurance. Regrettably his parents slept in another part of the house and his screams went unheard. The terror of this unconscious and collective source left Roger with a source of anxiety, a wound he is still trying to heal.

Jason had a domineering, critical father. From childhood on, he felt inadequate and lacked self esteem. Jason tried to compensate for this condition by living up to what his now dead father might have expected from him. He worked incessantly, both on the job and at home, the life of the typical over-achiever.

He had recurring dreams where he faced challenging or dangerous situations. Again and again he tried to tackle the task in the dream, only to wake up in deep fear without a resolution to the problem. When Jason began to recognize the nature of his problem, his dream scenario began to change. One of his late dreams had an authority figure, a physician, tell him that he would be subject to some throat and oral surgery. No reason for this invasive procedure was offered and Jason did not feel sick. As the dream came to an end, Jason walked away from the doctor's office, by himself, in what he knew was the right direction.

Here childhood and youth experiences were offered by the psyche for re-evaluation. With some help, Jason freed himself from old and no longer valid perceptions. His dreams, first with deep urgency, then with ever greater clarity let him free himself from obsolete imprints.

Albert was a high school student in Amsterdam when the Germans invaded his country and occupied it. His parents, prosperous Jewish merchants were openly worried about Nazi extermination camps targeting the local Jewish community. The very day Albert graduated from high school he packed some vital belongings while his parents were at work and he left home. He headed south into the more rural part of the country and found a friendly farmer offering him a bed and food in exchange for his labor. Albert survived the war and when the Allies liberated Amsterdam, he returned to the city of his birth. Fearing the worst, he went to his former home, now occupied by people he had never seen before. When he asked about the prior owners, he was told that they had been apprehended by the Nazis and had not returned.

Albert had recurring dreams of having killed someone and being pursued by a mysterious enemy. Sometimes he was caught, and his dream ended with him trying to defend his murder, a murder he could not recall. Other times he ran and ran, never reaching an end of his escape.

Here the conscious and unconscious together piled guilt on Albert for having survived, while his parents perished. Uncovering the guilt and recognizing that his escape was a rational action ultimately calmed Albert.

Dreams do not lie. They offer real and relevant messages. The message may be a pointer at something we have consciously overlooked. The dream says that what IT offers also is true and with varying degrees of urgency tells us to pay attention.

Most dreams involve us, with us experiencing what is happening and with us having reactions to the events. Other people may represent both us and outsiders inviting an objective interpretation of what they say and do. Those "others" may also represent a side of us. A side of us which wants to be recognized. In short, the entire cast of a dream calls for both a subjective and an objective interpretation.

We like to compare Jung's concept of "individuation" to growth. Exploring the unconscious and increasing awareness of our entire psyche can be fostered through dream interpretation. We encourage you to let dreams flow and to keep a dream booklet. Regrettably what happens during the night is easily forgotten in the morning. But your dream journal, when kept over time, will offer you fascinating insight into YOUR own psychic progress.

Elizabeth, 62, dreamt about being once again in the apartment she first occupied right after her marriage. Workmen were busy cutting space in a wall and installing a huge window. This window incredibly large, its height from the main floor all the way to the top, two storeys up. As the men struggled with the oversized pane, and finally put it in its place, Elizabeth noted piles of dirt and dust which had accumulated over many years in the old building. As she looked for housekeeping tools to remove the old dirt, she once more marveled at the expanse of light coming in through the glass.

This fine dream shows clearly that Elizabeth has drawn from the roots in her entire psyche and true growth has taken place. The translucent window indicating clarity, insight and understanding. Its size from the lowest level to the top, covering the entire mind. Dust and dirt, call it psychic rubble, is being swept up.

Daydreaming is a conscious process. It can be both escape and creation. It can be fantasy and inspire innovation. The colloquial use of calling someone a "dreamer" is derogatory referring to someone out of touch with reality. Our work with dreams is real, your investigation of your dreams is communicating with another part of YOU.

Interpersonal communications dominate our daily lives. "Failures to communicate" are a soap opera dilemma and "he does not understand me" is as common as "she does not listen to me".

The process of communicating can be dissected into two separate components. One is the process, the other the content. Complex models have been designed analyzing and deconstructing the process. A simplified structure might look something like this.

To begin with, we generate an idea which needs transmission to one or several others. Next we encode the idea. This means we put it into words, print or other means such as pictures, graphs or even physical items. Then we transmit the package. This could be orally, person to person, by mail or telephone, by fax or e-mail. Included in our transmission is our attitude and appearance, even physical action. Vital, at this point is that our total output is congruent. Our message will be misinterpreted if we smile when in fact we are angry. Here our delivery ends.

Now it is the receiver's turn. First of all, he must actually get  hold of our transmission, only then can he attempt to decode our bit of communication. If he stands in front of us, a verbal reply may be offered. Or he can read it, look at it, touch it or listen to it. Now, if we communicated successfully, the receiver will understand what and why we communicated. Most importantly, now he can formulate a response. His reaction is a point blank verification of our communication effectiveness.

It is obvious that "failures to communicate" can occur at any ONE of these junctures. Studies indicate that the most common miscues occur at both ends of the process. All too frequently our effort to get something across to someone else is badly managed. Our own motivation may be concealed. For instance we may dislike one of our coworkers for reasons and feelings which are not clear to us. Subsequently we may use a minor transgression on his part to read him the riot act, secretly hoping that our confrontation will make him quit. Furthermore our attack will release some of our built up hostility. Both items not conscious parts of the message.

In this case, what is called for is insight on our part. We need to be clear in our heads about WHAT we want to communicate. Is it ill feelings and dislike, or is it poor job performance?

Interpretation by the recipient leads to additional difficulties. You have heard some of the complaints like: " why the heck did they send a memo when all they needed to do is talk to me". "She left an angry message on my answering device, couldn't she be bothered to wait till I came back?" " I have No idea what they are talking about or want me to do". "Is it divorce, is THAT what you want?" " I am sorry Doctor Smith, but could you put this in language I can understand?" All of these reactions indicate a misalignment of intent versus perception.

In the end, what counts is the reaction to your communiqué. Success means that you got what you wanted. And what you desired may have been trivial. Then, should you have failed, you may let the issue rest. But on substantive items, a failure may call for some "negotiating", an issue we shall discuss a bit later.

Another interesting approach to communications is based on a "point" system. Should you pass a coworker in a hallway, you may offer a casual nod. This is a one pointer. If the passer by also nods, all is ok. No big deal, but harmony is confirmed. A two pointer would include some body language, say a smile or a casual "hello". Balance would call for a similar reply. Stopping for a chat merits three points and ever deeper involvement increases the number of points. What is important and valid in this system is balance. Imbalanced communications easily lead to misunderstanding and potential conflict.

A communications weapon is intentional unbalanced communication. It is a shock to the receiver and may result in what was wanted by the sender with minimal negotiating.

The content obviously is part and parcel of all processes discussed. It is crucial to construct communications so they can be understood by the receiver. This is a question of language and vocabulary. Common errors are "talking down" to the receiver, or the use of professional jargon. Also any message must make it clear what the recipient should do, and this includes that he should do nothing. "Let's have lunch sometime" may well mean "see you around".

A particularly dangerous sink hole is giving advice. Advice is given by everyone, especially by parents and superiors at work. From "let me tell you something" to "let me help you", the typical receiver of this well meant effort will respond negatively because advice is perceived as criticism. A colleague of ours loved to illustrate this dilemma by telling the story of the man who pulled a drowning man from the sea, who, as soon as he regained his breath, punched the rescuer on the chin.

Advice and help should only be offered when requested. Especially when it comes to our children, and we must remember that children remain so forever to their parents. Yet upbringing justifies a violation of our rule. Parents find it hard to recognize the end of the need to correct and improve offspring to their well proven standards. This is a true adult moment, calling for you to stop and look into your psychic mirror.

Personal interaction takes another hit with verbal finger pointing.

"You seem to think....you stated that....you continue to...." Such openings are simply called YOU messages which produce one consistent result, namely resistance. A far superior conversational approach rests on "I" messages. "I think that"...."I was told that"...."I understand you to say that". The "I" opens the door to dialogue. It leaves the respondent free to express his point of view without having to defend himself. The same way that a question facilitates a discussion and an answer closes it.

Social researchers have discovered that each one of us engages in about 200 meaningful negotiations per day. We tend to think of this process as something limited to unions or perhaps diplomats and business people. It is estimated that at least ten of the issues we handle may cause us psychic distress.

Your day may start with walking the dog to do his thing. He may pull this way to savor a special smell, you that way to the place where he likes to lift his leg. Generally you win in this contest because you have more power. What gives you an additional advantage is knowledge. You know his favorite spot to leave his mark. You still might lose the contest. A neighbor yells, the litter patrol gives you a ticket or your pooch leaves his dropping on your own lawn.

Children demand daily, perhaps constant negotiating. They want this, you want that. In this case more balance exists when compared to the dog example. Kids persist, wear you down, or get an ally. "Mom said". Or they bring in outside support like "other kids in my class don't have to…" even experts may enter the fray with "our teacher said…"

It does not end here. Spousal relations are a constant negotiating play. Here total power balance may well be in place. More and more it becomes evident that daily negotiating issues and their resolution can make or break key relationships and are central to our psychological well being.

Negotiations are not an end to themselves. They are a process. The end is getting what we want from other people. At first glance our objective is to win a debate or an argument, both essentially negotiations. The outcome, I win, you lose. The end result of this conclusion, however, is likely to be negative over the longer pull. Relationships will suffer. The loser will turn resentful. His anger will bring about an escalating conflict.

A far better result of any negotiation is a win-win outcome. I get what I want and you do too. It calls for an avoidance of advocacy and acceptance of a cooperative, mutual approach. Gathering information is essential to this process. Mutual understanding of the true issues under discussion is required. Frequently wrong assumptions and false issues are turned into hot items leading to a breakdown. The correct approach avoids ultimatums and a competitive climate. Conciliation is the goal, not a dead adversary.

Negotiations can break down. Take it or leave it, the final word. If you are given this ultimatum, you may decide to cut your loss and leave. But you can also decide to try and rebalance the power equation. You may be able to accomplish this by changing your position and providing a new basis for negotiation. Another method to change the climate is to find an ally, an outside supporter of your position, someone respected by your opponent.

When all is said and done, both parties are advised to positively reinforce their decisions. This act, akin to shaking hands after a fight, limits the possibility of what is called buyers remorse, the afterthought that you have been had.

## Chapter 5

# Under Control

These are difficult times. We often seem adrift in an ocean of uncertainty. The rate of change is ever accelerating. Technical innovation is passing many of us by. Global problems appear unmanageable. To put it bluntly, things, intentionally using this universal catch all, seem to be out of control.

Our language offers an interesting perspective to control. One is active and personal by applying the term: in control. The other is passive and refers to the object and is: under control.

We humans have sought some measure of control over our fate and fortune since our earliest days. Eternally, the future, and the security and safety we sought, have lain occluded. Our ancestors tried to pacify the Gods through sacrifices, including fellow humans. Before large battles, the entrails of sheep and chickens were carefully dissected in search of some good omen.

Uncertainty about our own future has fostered whole cottage industries engaged in fortune telling. Tea leaves, psychic readings, our own palms, cards, specifically Tarot Cards are among a multitude of media employed to foretell the future.

In reality the only moment we can attempt to control is right now. Now we can make a choice, not yesterday, not tomorrow. The past is behind us. We can attempt to influence the future with careful planning. Our health is influenced with preventive measures. We buy insurance and we save, all in an attempt to provide some control over our future security.

Philosophically a case can be made for not knowing the future. If we were aware of the disasters which may impact us at some point out there, our anticipation of this event would surely ruin the years in between.

For the collective, control serves us well. Organizations cannot function without some control. Order is required to reinforce a common purpose. From military to business organizations, power and control are applied to reach common goals. Individual expression is frequently subordinated to policy and orders from above.

The issue of power and control over other people is central to this discussion. Drawing from the non rational world we try to influence others via witchcraft, voodoo and by casting spells. From an animalistic perspective, control is viewed as a male instinct. Men are supposed to be in control. This control is translated into power over others, the power to make them do what we want them to do. This relationship can get very complex with obedience required in the military, yet an employee, subject to the bosses' demands, still is a volunteer with the right to quit, if he feels abused.

Controlling others because of a power imbalance leads to trouble. The controlled subject may obey and perform because he has to. He does not offer loyalty or love in return. Hostility and rebelliousness are imbedded in the relationship. A far superior approach to imbalance can be found in the negotiating paragraphs of the previous chapter

Psychologically we walk in turgid waters when we relate control to feelings and the emotional realm in general. "Get a hold of yourself ! "

How often have we heard this admonition from others. And how often have we pleaded with ourselves trying to regain control over our emotions run amok. Typically what has overpowered us is anger turned to rage and fear blown into terror. These emotions are real, they are you. But they prevent you from any attempt to manage the problem causing your upset. This is the moment for you to draw on your natural strengths and let them help you evaluate the facts at your disposal.

We recommend an analytical system which you might consider and use again and again when psychological upset bothers you. It will calm you and may offer solutions to your problem. First of all, step back and as soberly as possible analyze the situation, the rational facts and the emotions swirling around it. Then try and isolate the central issues and determine what you can do about whatever change is called for to reduce conflict. Next select both the best rational and emotional approaches which you hope will provide an improvement. Here it is important to focus on a step by step attack. Big problems defy simple solutions. If necessary, inch your way along the road to progress. Your patience may be rewarded with incremental success. Implementation of your best ideas must be followed with a careful review of the outcome. Was it what you had hoped for? What went right, what did not? This final step of a managed and rational approach to problem solving will now give you hints if additional moves are called for.

The concept of keeping your emotions under control may have negative consequences also. Sandra was the ultimate calm person. She showed no emotion, either positive or negative. In fact she had no feelings. Her entire emotional life lay dormant. She was bothered by this inability to feel and by some irritating psychosomatic symptoms. These symptoms, she felt, were caused by feelings she should experience, but could not. It took some time for her to let her think about and remember her youth which was dominated by a hypercritical mother. Nothing Sandra did would please her mother. This constant lack of approval, and what Sandra felt as absence of love, was a deep and lasting pain for the young girl. The only way Sandra found to deal with this disappointment was to repress all feelings. She built a wall around painful memories and experiences, putting them in storage so to speak. But her mind and her body did not permit the denial of sad feelings and subsequently all feelings. One day she broke down into a flood of tears, and they all came back.

Psychological distress, that dreaded out of control feeling may occur when you are by yourself. Thoughts and negative emotions tumbling non stop with a nagging feeling that you are going crazy. You may be obsessed with thoughts about a stressful situation, perhaps your health, or your job, perhaps your marriage. You may seek comfort in some compulsive activity. Food or drink are common outlets for this seemingly uncontrollable desire.

Fighting with yourself by yourself is a difficult task. Getting feedback and confirmation from others is recommended. Sharing problems a is good approach to calming psychic storms. Cognitive activity on your part, using your reasoning power, another first aid step leading to long term repair.

There is no solution to what appears to be a loss of control. We yearn for predictability, certainty and minimal change. As stress and pressure increase, as uncertainty rises to anxiety, we all must focus on those aspects of our lives where we can exert some control and attempt to dismiss those beyond our sphere of influence. The flippant NMR, "Not My Responsibility" should become one of your survival tools.

## Chapter 6

# Worry...Anxiety...Fear...Panic

We see this chain as a continuum, not as separate psychic disturbances. The concepts are akin to a rubber band stretching ever thinner and closer to rupture, the closer we get to the panic level. Diagnosis, in our case self diagnosis, is step one to understanding and coping with psychological difficulties which prevent us from leading a full life. In everyday language, even when used by therapists, worry, anxiety, fear and panic are often muddled and used interchangeably. To help you identify what bothers you, we will try and limit the overlap of these phenomena as much as possible.

Worry, we propose, is dominated by our conscious mind. We tend to worry about real, hands-on matters. " Why are we broke again?" "Why are the kids still outside in the dark?" "Is that lump a boil or something cancerous?" "Why did the boss look at me askance?" "What are they doing to clean up our polluted air?" "Why do I worry all the time?" "Am I dressed right for the occasion?" "Where are my notes for the presentation?"

These questions illustrate that worry is generally identifiable. It is not nebulous or floating. Yet it is a very complex phenomenon. The sample questions make it clear that worry is focused on the future. It is anticipatory. But it also draws on our past, on some negative experience which raises a red flag about a possible repetition. To make things worse, we add a dash of imagination painting a mental picture of a worst possible outcome. If we get emotional on top of this explosive mixture, worry can become poisonous.

We all know "worry-warts". Some of us are more sensitive to uncertainty. Then there are pessimists and optimists. We speculate about future outcomes in different ways. But all of us can attempt to gain a measure of control by isolating those tormenting "What If" thoughts and subjecting them to rigorous analysis.

Using our definition, to begin with, we can scan the outside. What are the facts at our disposal. Where, precisely does uncertainty creep in. Does this uncertainty really involve a risk. What are the odds of a negative outcome. Do the odds require attention or action. If yes, what can we, and what should we do. This chain of rational appraisal should lead to the identification of a possible threat which can be addressed with action. Action, if called for, replaces stress and worry. This entire process can be enhanced by asking for advice and support from others.

Most worries are defused and laid to rest when scrutinized by our thinking ability. The worried speaker who feels under-prepared can bone up. The mother who has lost her children can make a few phone calls and try and locate them....and set rules for the future. The environmentalist can join others who are similarly concerned, and he can trade in his gas guzzler for a hybrid car.

Anxiety, this negative anticipation of the future has deeper roots. Not only does this symptom typically originate in our past, even childhood, but is lodged in the lowest depth of our minds, in the unconscious. Anxiety is based on experience, it is learned. On the positive side, this also means that it can be unlearned.

The causes for anxiety can find their origin in a number of experiences which at the time were found to be highly threatening. And at this time we were not prepared to evaluate the severity of the danger, our youth and inexperience being the limiting factors.

A common cause which we identified was an unexpected loss. Sarah's mother went on a lengthy vacation when Sarah was only four months old. She was farmed out to a grandmother who took good care of her, but the sudden absence of her mother's warmth and mother's milk carved a permanent scar. From this specific example we can generalize that the frightened self originates in infancy and childhood. The broad causes are a loss or a lack of love, a meaningful separation, loss of security and protection, all of them at the base of our pyramid of needs. When the very foundation of our survival needs is threatened, anxiety is born.

Anxiety has its origins in what at the time were perceived as traumatic events. Habitual anxiety is called "general anxiety disorder". It is the feeling that something terrible is going to happen to us. Usually it is not a real danger, but the thought about a potential danger. This inner voice warns us that unless we get and stay vigilant, disaster will strike. Now the anxious person is in a double bind. Getting and being ever vigilant becomes a sort of disaster insurance. Since nothing bad does happen to us most of the time, being anxious is felt to be a barrier to misfortune.

Our perceptions and our memories are personal. They are the very I, the total you. In fact, they may not represent reality. Most certainly they do not always concur with the views of others. Therefore can we trust our perceptions, or should we allow ourselves to use every recall as a REFRAME. This means re-interpreting events and reviewing our reactions to them. Casting doubt on the validity of anxiety is step one to overcoming it.

Many who suffer from anxiety have a tendency to catastrophize. This is an automatic escalation process with no end to the downward spiral. An ingrown toenail leads to imagined surgery and a following staph infection with the whole foot needing amputation. By now the psyche of the anxious person is in turmoil. Ultimately, the fear of death is a constant companion of the anxiety victim.

Highly emotional events are stored in us permanently. "Forget it" is impossible. There is no delete key. Our storage capacity is immense and both our minds and our bodies serve as disk drives, so to speak. Overload is a common result. We pay for unexpressed and unresolved experiences with symptoms, psychosomatic illness. Once more we need to emphasize that these sensations are real, not imagined. But real in the sense that they are a manifestation of emotional upheaval, not a physiological breakdown. Here the anxious person may fall victim to an unending chain by searching internally in full alert for symptoms, and when found or even created, react with double alarm. This fearful attention makes the symptoms more and more frightening. Ultimately the victim may perceive a loss of psychic or physical functioning possibly leading to outright terror.

It is essential for the anxious personality to view psychosomatic symptoms for what they are: a message. It would be helpful if they had voices and could tell us about the content and purpose of the blowup. Dreams may offer insight in this discovery process. Exploring negative feelings also may offer clues to where a new understanding is needed. The particular part of the body that is afflicted may be symbolic of the struggle. As an example, a migraine forces the individual to withdraw and look after himself, instead of others.

The resolution of anxiety disorder could hinge on the discovery and disarming of the original painful experience. This could well involve protracted therapy. A lengthy procedure might reinforce a feeling of pathology, of being mentally out of balance, in the anxious person. It is too late to recreate the feeling of self assurance and reassurance lost in childhood. The moment when a father promised to support the first try at swimming, but failed. The time when a mother promised to be home by five, but came in late at eight. These events mold the mind and give the anxious person no choice but to anticipate surprises when there are none. The self confident individual, in turn, reacts to a perceived threat only when it occurs.

We suggest that anxiety be approached as another manageable experience. This is an attempt at becoming a bystander to anxiety. Literally live with it and through it. This is an analytical process to determine what caused our attack. We must try and be as specific and timely as possible. When did our feelings get aroused and why. Was it a rekindling of an old hurt? As we stated before, that offers the moment for reframing, re-evaluating and defusing the perceived danger. The base for safety and security lies in self confidence with trust in others and getting reassurance and support from those important to us.

A particular version of anxiety are phobias. Here fear is mixed into unreasonable anxiety. The widely known claustrophobia is the anxiety tied to feeling closed in. Another fairly common example is agoraphobia, the anxiety tied to leaving the safety of home. There are those who suffer from fear of heights, flying, suspension bridges or tunnels. The list is endless since phobias are personal and based on a frightening experience so devastating, that any repetition of the event causes dire anxiety.

We used the word unreasonable to label phobias since those of us who have observed a victim, know that the perceived worrisome situation in fact is not a threat. Those in pain can be helped. Repetitive exposure under guidance from a trusted person will heal the sufferer. The mind can be reconditioned. Ultimately the painful event causing the phobia will be defused and the automatic reaction abolished.

Fear is a natural reaction to evident danger. Frequent reference is made to the "fight or flight" response as a reaction to a serious threat. When facing a mammoth, our ancestors had to make a choice in order to survive, either fight the monstrous animal, or run for their lives. In short, fear is a survival instinct. Fear caused by external events arouses us and gets us to react appropriately.

A different issue arises when we are subjected to fear caused by psychological and psychosomatic threats. Panic attacks are a prime example for internally caused upheaval with catastrophic fear as a result.

Jim recalls many nightmares from his childhood. He was much closer to his mother than his father and was what was then called a sensitive child. He had his first full fledged panic attack when he was twelve. He remembers his feeling of having lost all control and thought that he was near death. Put to bed, he was shaking and shivering with his mother hovering over him. His father had left the room, shaking his head. No one had any idea of what was wrong with him. After about an hour he regained some composure. The family physician, when consulted the next day, prescribed heavy doses of calcium. From that day on Jim associated going to bed with catastrophic anxiety, now identified as panic attacks.

Panic attacks come on unexpectedly and quickly. Typical symptoms are dizziness, a feeling of unreality, hyperventilation, the fear of going crazy, racing pulse and in some cases, loss of consciousness. This happened to Jim twice in later years. Each time he was rushed by ambulance to the emergency room with a suspected heart attack. In both of these cases, his blood pressure had dropped to shock levels. His recovery from a critical state to a near normal one was rapid in each instance. But his deep fear, of what he learned were panic attacks, remained. Jim's account of this torture was that it was not a near death experience, but coming back from death.

Panic is connected to the fear of fear. Our body has become our enemy, as has our mind. The first step to recovery calls for the recognition that the physical symptoms are not life threatening. In fact they are non physiological and are created by our own psyche. The realization that both the psychosomatic uproar and the psychic storm, are no real danger ultimately reduces the fear of the sufferer. This is step one to full recovery.

Healing panic attacks requires courage. The persistence to live through the events as they occur. A diligent confrontation of symptoms slowly results in their disappearance. This is once again a cognitive function, analyzing and reasoning. The experience of fewer and milder attacks brings confirmation of success, another boost to the victim's will and power of control.

## Chapter 7

# Get Mobilized

Most of us, if not all of us have had an anxious moment or experienced temporary depression. Sociologists provide the staggering information that nearly one out of four of us in all modern societies suffers from prolonged depression. And the older we are, the more likely it is that we are afflicted.

A multitude of symptoms are the companions of depression. In general, the lust for life is gone. Nothing is pleasurable or interesting. The sufferer feels hopeless, worthless and is always tired. Thoughts of death occupy his mind and suicide seems to offer a way out.

The depressed has lost his physical strength and feels incompetent, even at work. He may gain weight, or lose it. Alcohol may become a source of temporary comfort. The overall mood is pessimistic.

In our experience depression is a reaction, a defense against unexpressed and undigested overpowering feelings. These may be rage, grief, fear, worry or a deep personal loss. The result, a near absence of feeling, a dulling of the inner emotional life.

Childhood trauma has been identified as a frequent cause for depression, particularly chronic cases. Long term physical pain is another cause in this category.

Sally sought help suffering from flat line depression. She came across as dull, lifeless, juiceless and was not forthcoming. Yet she functioned. She held a job which took all the output she could generate. Her social life was meager and she was unable to maintain longer term relationships. When she lost her job and casual date at the same time, she knew she needed help.

Sally was Catholic and perceived her suffering as God's will. She had five sisters and when her favorite died of cancer at an early age, she again saw it as destiny. Life was beyond control, Sally felt utterly powerless. Her fate was handed out to her and she was conditioned to take it.

Clearing her chronic case of depression required a deep look into her childhood. This involved a rediscovery of severe abuse at home and at the Catholic school at the hands of the nuns. She spent her youth not just frightened, but in a permanent state of terror. Her solution was to make herself as invisible as possible and by turning off all feelings.

Her therapy was long and based on her discovery of her own abilities. She literally woke up to life, re-thought her experiences and the present. She took  hold of it and got mobilized. She took charge, got married and had a daughter whom she loved. As she grew stronger and stronger, she entered college, graduated and took a challenging and responsible position involving frequent contact with the public. Her interest now general and focused on family, marriage and work. Her abilities giving her satisfaction.

A case of acute and temporary depression involved Martha. Her paternalistic husband, a prominent executive, died within a few months after having been diagnosed for thyroid cancer. Martha had been a devoted, if not subservient wife and the loss sapped her energy and will to live. Since she was unable to regain her footing for months on end, she sought help.

It took little time to discover that the loss of her husband had doubled the pain and grief of a prior experience. One of Martha's brothers, one she was very close to, had died years earlier. This, a loss she had buried and which now came to the fore with twice the impact. Here a current event triggered and revitalized an old issue, and together they created a crisis.

Martha's discoveries freed her and she found herself. Her mobilization found expression in creativity and artistic work. This life, her own life, had been waiting to be discovered and when it was, her depression receded.

Carl was the CEO of a large national corporation which had a policy of compulsory retirement at age 65. A few months after his involuntary step out of his career, Carl sank into deep depression. Having been stripped of his stature, his purpose, his routine and his person to person work contacts left him adrift. He had made no plans about what to do with himself, having "been too busy" to think about it.

Carl's recovery was rapid. His energy was rekindled when he joined two active groups, one charitable, the other pseudo administrative as a board member of the local hospital. Pleasure was added to his palette with vacation travel to places he had previously visited for business purposes only. He discovered art and became active in the local museum's activities.

Carl's solution involved several general approaches to overcoming depression. He remained active, joined groups for social contact, he continued to be useful and involved. Perhaps most importantly he had fun, he spoiled himself so to speak. "With the few years I have left", he said, "why not".

Both chronic and acute depression may have their roots in trauma based on past experience. Common issues were framed in childhood, others are connected to family problems, abuse, health, money problems and living conditions. These impressions tend to foster automatic reactions in the depressed. "It won't work", "no use trying", "that's no good" are such preconditioned reactions.

Digging out the past and confronting the present offer solutions to depression. Exercise on a routine basis helps overcome inertia. Re-energizing ourselves takes courage and determination. Giving up and surrendering lead to failure. As we succeed with new activities, new interests and new social connections, we should measure our progress and reward ourselves with little pleasures. Doing better, doing well, is easily recognized by others. Our own view of ourselves and of our recovery is central to regaining optimism and containing our depression.

## Chapter 8

# Annoyance, Anger, Rage

Once again we follow a progressive line of similar emotions from low impact to near catastrophic levels. Day in day out we all get annoyed and irritated by events which go counter to our expectations. We ourselves can be the target of this emotion. We lost our glasses again or the keys to the car have disappeared. Our frustration with our own memory rings a bell when a familiar face has lost its name. There are hundreds of daily occasions when we are challenged and annoyed by the world around us. The bus is late, the security inspector at the airport gives you the total once over, the dog refuses to do his thing and it is raining, your wife has put your socks in the wrong drawer again, your son has once more produced mediocre grades and your favorite TV program has been preempted by a fund raiser. Count the times. It seems to be a constant invasion of negative input. And where is the relief valve to let off built up steam?

Constant low levels of irritation can result in stress and its plethora of symptoms. Yet, most of the time, we manage. Our complex mental filtering system of memories, feelings, reasoning and habitual or preconditioned responses lets us absorb the constant tiny stings of daily life. We tend to able to forgive and even forget annoyances.

Anger presents a very different picture. At first blush, anger is a social taboo. People who display anger are behaviorally out of tune. We disagree. Anger is part of all of us and has been made unacceptable through mores, manners  and religion. Yet, coming back to the "fight or flight" syndrome, it requires anger to chose the fight choice. For generations, going back to our primitive ancestors, collective anger was used to motivate fearful humans to attack a dangerous adversary. Might this be another tribe or a ferocious animal.

Another, equally important venue where anger had and has social validity relates to dominance and social structure. We all have seen the dominance ritual of primates, all involving displays of anger and implied threat making the  point of who is in charge. Pep talks are a normal warm up procedure before American football games. A team leader tries to create a winning spirit with fierceness and anger. Together, let's get them, the theme. The same method is used in all military operations involving danger. Firing up the troops reinforces leadership and creates team spirit.  Anger is successfully used as a personal and social tool, as it has been for ages.

Anger is turbo charged annoyance. Our blood is beginning to boil. We see red. Anger is our reaction to a severe provocation. We have been insulted or denigrated. Our opponent has been disrespectful of us or what we represent. Or maybe he broke normal behavioral standards. Perhaps we perceive ourselves as the victims of an unreasonable attack. Our pride, our self respect, our feelings are at stake. All of this occurs as interpreted by us, unfiltered by reason or outside points of view.

Most common occurrences for anger to arise are at home, with our children and our mates. Next in frequency is our work environment. Both situations provide all too many opportunities where the other side is "not listening", in reality meaning they are not doing what we want them to do. Some popular specific causes for uproar are politics, money, who is the boss and personal insults.

Anger puts us in a double bind. As we pointed out, it is a legitimate emotion. But contemporary religious, societal and behavioral standards require us to put a lid on it. Even more rationale is offered by psychological insights which support the concept that demonstrating anger is counter productive. It breeds resentment, hostility, resistance and polarizes the opponents.

Another complication arises with the build up of anger over time. Daily we suppress anger into the unconscious. Being well mannered or in an inferior position forces us to swallow anger on an ongoing basis. Regrettably we all lack opportunities to drain this buildup off, bit by bit. All too frequently alcohol tends to pop the cork and the ensuing explosion is ill timed, is launched without a valid cause and results in bad feelings all around. Our capacity to forgive, though it might be useful, is diminished.

Only one valid conclusion can be drawn from the above, we must control our anger outbursts, even though they may seem justified. When we feel the blood pressure rising…. we must STOP right then and let our thinking take over. This is the moment to ask ourselves if demonstrated anger would change the situation. Consider the possibility that we are the cause of the conflict. What did we do or say to bring about the barrier. What caused the loss of normal contact. Are feelings involved or are there substantive issues which block normal communications.

Cool off. The calm person is in control. Realize that most likely anger will not create the desired change. If you are in charge, you can decide to discuss the issue further, or to let it go as not being worth the trouble. Even if provoked, staying calm tells the other side that you will not take the bait. Your conscious awareness that you are angry lets you decide whether to express it or not. Calming and controlling yourself and containing anger consciously, will make you ever stronger in conflict situations.

Daniel belonged to the local golf and country club. Saturday evening dinner at the club had become a routine. Dan had spent the morning rechecking the books of his company. His review confirmed that he lost money during the past month. He was still upset when he arrived for his dinner date. He had his "usual", two dry martinis before the meal. "I'll have another one", he said when he placed his meal order. The food was slow in coming, the dining room filled with guests. When his steak arrived, he cut into it and found that it was cooked through and through, not rare as ordered. Dan  hailed the Maitre D' to his table with a brisk gesture and shouted "look at this damn steak, will ya. A shoe sole. Lousy cooking, lousy service, I wonder why anybody comes to eat here, take the damn thing back." All the guests at nearby tables had stopped eating and were watching the performance. Without saying a word, the Maitre D' removed the inedible insult and silence fell over the room. When Bob received his month's bill from the club, it included a note signed by three directors notifying him that his membership had been cancelled for "inappropriate behavior".

Claude, a six foot two French expatriate had reserved three bulkhead seats in economy class for himself and his coworkers for the long flight from Paris to Chicago. When he checked in he was told that his seats had been reassigned to a woman with two small children. "But I was confirmed, and look all three of us are tall and need the extra space", he growled at the agent. "We are sorry sir, but we had to make the change. We'll do the best to seat you gentlemen together", was the response. Claude shrugged his shoulders and gave his colleagues a disgusted smile. "Ok, please try" finished the conversation. When the trio lined up to board, Claude was presented with three no charge upgrades to business class.

At the end of our scale, and in fact off the page, is rage. It has been suggested that we all carry a load of repressed, unconscious rage based on childhood misery and other internal conflicts. (Sarno) The seeds of this repressed material then sprout into psychosomatic flowers later on, something we discussed earlier. The rage we cover now is the violent explosion of anger. It is uncontrolled anger.

We all are familiar with road rage when a usually minor transgression results in violence. Driving can be stressful, commuting in endless, slow moving lines is frustrating and has its own etiquette. If this is violated, anger is produced. Cursing, light flashing and finger gestures abound. When the thin band of patience breaks, physical violence results. The desire to get revenge overpowers reason.

Domestic rage, commonly referred to as abuse, is another recognized phenomenon. Normally it is caused by the man in the household who resorts to physical violence to vent his frustration. Both children and women are the victims.

A somewhat novel version of rage is sports rage. Typically this involves groups, if not mobs of "sports fans" who trash anything in front of them. The normally low key British spectators have become famous for mob violence in the stadium. In the US too, it is now occurring that unpopular people on the field, might they be players or umpires, get pelted with trash and bottles. This phenomenon has a sociological impetus. A loss of inhibition and restraints supported by group behavior and primed by alcohol.

Our advice to those who might be rage prone is twofold. If and when your anger wants to boil over, lock yourself into a room, by yourself. Come out only after you have fully regained your composure. Once you have admitted to yourself that you are rage prone: seek professional help. You need it. There is no other way.

## Chapter 9

# Loss and Grieving

Daily we are exposed to small losses and little gains. On the whole these pluses and minuses balance out. Even if they do not, the human psyche is magnificently flexible and "we manage". Only when we get run over by a serious loss, then we need help, from both internal and external sources.

Mac lost his brother in a terrible car accident. He seemed to cope. When asked about the origin of his strength, he noted, "I have good defenses".

He added that his father put in place both rational and irrational strengths which allowed him to deal with anxiety and loss. "I trusted dad", he said. "He made me feel secure and safe. He was there when there was trouble. It was not a hit and miss situation, there was continuity. I grew up counting on it. I'll never forget the day when I found a small dead songbird in our garden. It was a Sunday and dad was home. I called him and he told me about death, what it was and that we all would succumb to it some day. Even you will, he said to me, but that should not happen for a long time. Now let's bury the little bird, let's give him his own little grave to rest in". Facing loss and understanding it helped Mac develop a feeling of being ok about both himself and the world around him. And when adversity struck, he was able to deal with it.

Our childhood is laced with losses which, at the time, we are all too often unable to understand or digest. We lack the experience and reasoning to put them in perspective. The experience of abandonment is etched into our psyches. We are left, seemingly alone to cope on our own. These memories can act as tyrants in our future. As infants we may scream as a reaction to perceived loss. As adults our societal mores demand more control. What are we to do with our losses then?

And severe losses pile up as we age. The death of a loved person becomes a recurrent event. The loss of a pet, a dog or a cat, has an equally painful impact. The object of our love may be other than human. It can be inanimate, perhaps a painting stolen by robbers. It may be an idealized concept, losing an emotionally charged election or a war. A beautiful woman may lose her good looks and go into deep mourning. One of our own daughters grieved when we sold the house she was born in. Our own death looms at some unpredictable juncture. Anticipatory grieving about this inevitability is one of the causes of depression in older people. As the end nears, depression and self pity go arm in arm.

When children grow up and leave the house, suddenly many mothers lose their purpose in life. "I feel as though

I've lost my job" said one woman as her youngest child left for college. For all of us careers come to an end with retirement. Our stature, our self esteem are seriously eroded. The very events which happen to us carve away at our carefully built self defenses. Our losses over time seem to become cumulative. Freud suggested that some of our attachments to love objects are permanent and that the pain of their loss endures.

We engage in all sorts of games to stave off the pain of loss. We anticipate that the worst will happen, then if it does, we are prepared. The mirror of this move is to predict that nothing good will come to fruition, and disappointment is avoided thereby. The fear of loss can become a weapon against loss. If we are afraid and nothing bad happens, fear becomes the equivalent of an insurance policy against loss. Superstitious and magic acts and amulets are used to avoid disaster. Knock on wood, carry a rabbit's foot, a shamrock or a lucky charm are all designed to spare us pain.

We feel especially threatened when a contemporary dies. The older we get, the more carefully we read the obituary pages. There, but for the grace of God, go I, is a normal reaction. This kind of anticipation and preparation is both good and bad. It does build our defenses, but can also lead to depression and melancholia.

One common method of dealing with a loss is denial, feeling that it simply did not take place. Some deeply religious people have the capacity to move the lost person to Heaven, or some other tangible place and stay in contact with the lost one there. Grave sites are the equivalent of a permanent presence and do provide comfort.

Mourning is the process of allowing yourself to be distressed. It is the first essential move to accepting the reality of a loss. Sometimes this acceptance tests our resolve and strength when we have to deal with suicide, murder or another version of "senseless" death.

Grieving is the proper discharge of built up sorrow. This can be silent sadness, crying, weeping and wailing. We tend to mourn where it is safe or "normal" to do so. Coming to terms with the loss is hindered by the repression of feelings or a fear of becoming overwhelmed by our powerful emotions.

Sharing the loss is very helpful to being able to bear it. Support from others is, we believe, essential. Humanity offers pity, empathy and sympathy as aids to the bereaved. The German language has a unique concept in the word "Mitleid". It literally means being sorry with some one.

In case of a death, a funeral provides a suitable event for some closure, some equanimity. A current societal emphasis is placed on "closure". This may never occur. But we are improving when our loss turns into a significant and not unpleasant memory. Genuine closure occurs when we are able to form new connections, new relationships to replace the old ones.

# Chapter 10

# Love and Marriage

Love American style all too often is a soap opera brought to life. Marriageable perfection is seen in great sex, large breasts, a nice car, lots of money, a perfect body and good looks. We both love animals, she is such a good listener, we both want lots of kids, our marriage is going to be a 50-50 relationship, illustrate another umbrella under which vows are exchanged. Love is given expression as a hunger for affection. "I need" takes precedence over "I give", which becomes a duty. What is not obvious to the participants is that all of this initial enthusiasm is perishable. What is overlooked is that love is something you feel, not something you do.

Another set is based on "the two of us against the world". Young people who bring a load of hardship from a difficult childhood, a lack of support and security, even abuse, tend to look for someone with whom a defensive alliance can be formed.

We all bring our own set of baggage to our marriage. And most of this luggage goes past the security screeners, unopened and un-inspected. Worse, much of the concealment is intentional. We want to be saleable, we want to look good. Wisdom finds expression in the saying that love is not gazing at each other, but looking outward, together, in the same direction.

Marriage is the most difficult relationship we enter in life. The two participants ostensibly are strangers. Perhaps they went to school together, perhaps they dated in college, but at the base, they are free agents trying to work very, very closely together for the rest of their lives. The obvious conclusion: look before you leap.

One generalization has stood the test of time. Marriage partners with similar backgrounds and similar interests have one leg up on making their union a success. Freud suggested that the choice of a partner should bubble up from the unconscious. Perhaps here a dream might be a guide, but who, in the heat of the pursuit has the time and patience to seek out an analyst to help dig out unconscious needs and assets.

Carl Jung recognizes that the instinctive choices we tend to make are not necessarily bad. Such unconscious relationships are based on the preservation of the species and are biological. The young married display a childlike happiness. In addition their motivation to marry is influenced heavily by parental influences, especially the young man's relationship to his mother and the woman's to her father. Certain voids or strengths detected in a parent need to be filled or avoided and is taken into account. The resulting process moves along unconsciously.

Consciousness, Jung proposes, arises naturally during the second half of life. The partners who entered into marriage without prior exploration of their personalities, their respective egos, a recognition of who they are as individuals, fall into a trap. They progress from passion (I want) to duty (I must) to burden and ultimately to discontent (I want change). Partners who can go through these transformations together and in harmony, can form what Jung calls a conscious marriage.

Another aspect of Jung's deliberations concerns our need to seek fulfillment of certain images. Specifically he refers us to the anima, the perfect image of woman carried in all men, and the animus, the all-man hero carried in all women. Frequently a marriage partner becomes the vessel into whom the other projects either the anima or animus. Such projections need to become conscious. Failing this recognition, should one partner reject or fail to live up to the projection, the relationship is in danger.

We have found what should be discussed before sealing the deal are reality issues like, interests, ambitions, goals, philosophy and yes, religion. What are our music and literary interests, can we talk openly with each other and accept each other's reality. This applies to both thinking issues and feelings. How are we creative, are we inquisitive, reflective or analytical. These points form the basis of our communications.

Specifically can we create some mutuality on such issues as each other's career, where to live, what to buy, what to do for fun, what to save and, right from the start, how many children we want and how to handle rearing them. This short list is critical. In our work we have found that unexpressed differences on this list lead later to serious difficulties. Additionally we must recognize that change is constant, and when one partner alters his view of one of the central points of a relationship, the equilibrium will be tilted, perhaps terminally.

All this may sound unemotional and cold. We know that data gathering and data processing, almost working like a computer, is the correct preparation for a solid relationship. Of course this includes feelings, their expression, both warm and cold.

It is far riskier to typecast a promising match for either sex. A self assured and confident partner ranks high on the positive scale. This trait is not to be confused with arrogance or braggadocio. The confident partner will see little need to seek dominance in the relationship. The previously mentioned 50-50 partnership, if taken literally, is stale. It rests on compromise, not on mutual growth and gain.

A readiness and willingness to say "let's do it", is favorable, if not necessary. This commitment should find expression in concern for the partner, an investment in the relationship. A realistic approach to each other's strengths and weaknesses avoids later disappointment based on idealizing certain characteristics.

True feelings should be divulged. Being truthful in this sense does not mean being critical or judgmental, thus hurting the feelings of the partner based on the assumption of being up front. The discussion of feelings provides the opportunity for mutual gain since our own experiences are just that, our own. Sharing them therefore enriches both partners. But marriage can produce extreme

emotions and expression of chaotic feelings which can cause distress in the relationship.

Disagreements, even conflicts are unavoidable. Listening does not require concurrence or submission. But hearing the partner with all senses, from words to body language is based on keeping an open mind. Criticism, being a "you" message may produce negative reactions. A better approach of venting a problem is a complaint in the form of an "I" statement. The good partner understands and manages his ill feelings and seeks to re-establish trust in both parties.

Certain traits have been found to forecast trouble in marital relationships. Many are the opposite of what we found to promote a good marriage. A partner who feels and acts superior is blatantly arrogant. Strengths should be used as an asset, not a weapon. Put-downs can be fatal.

A clutching partner, one who wants to be together at all times, is afraid to be left, is jealous and requires constant reassurance is fearing failure of the relationship. A failure he is likely to produce thereby.

The opposite personality, the one who does not want to give up all freedoms of single life, another failure in waiting. Relinquishing certain freedoms and "assumed rights" promotes trust between the partners.

Change is inevitable. Yes, marriage is a contract with an assortment of assumptions, some accepted mutually as valid, others as flexible guidelines, some as old fashioned nonsense. As the participants change, as the relationship takes on new dimensions, there are two options. One of the partners may cry "foul" and trouble looms. Now one of the partners may take the occasion to offer the ultimatum of "this is the way I am, take it or leave it". The other choice calls for an adjustment to change, an abolition of rigid absolutes. This step might be followed by an effort aimed at complementary change. Then both players can meet at a new level, an agreeable middle ground.

Typically what goes wrong is a shattering of illusions on which a marriage was based. Sex becomes routine or is abandoned altogether. I love you is no longer said, but sent by mail in mass produced cards. The words "always" and "never" enter discussions and arguments. So does the label "you" instead of the "I" which should be offered as a conversation opener. Children are in trouble and one parent gets the blame for their failure. One of the partners, probably approaching middle age, wonders if this is really all there is to life. "If only" becomes the expression of what appears to be a life wasted.

Roughly 50% of all marriages in America crash on the rocks of these and other change based problems. Before this happens, the partners should ask for help. This is not sign of weakness, since a thoughtful outsider may be able to help defuse the imminent crisis. Marriage is not a trap in perpetuity. The contractual part of the agreement may have been shattered by infidelity and change in one of the partners may be indigestible by the other.

Divorce is the final solution, but not an easy one. All too often the legal proceedings are bitter and protracted. Animosity, if not hatred become part of the dissolution. If children are involved, they too will suffer from the breakup. One of the parents will be put into a part time, subordinate role. A step parent may fill in the void, but the loss of the real parent leaves a scar.

A frequent complaint from divorcees is loneliness. Old friends made by the couple tend to fall away, or ally themselves with only one of the former partners. Financial solutions of divorces may impose hardship and insecurity on one or both participants. Marriage is a major psychological investment, divorce is therefore perceived as a failure. Perhaps worst of all, divorce means starting the whole game all over again.

Pregnancy is an enormous responsibility which must be acknowledged by both the prospective father and mother. We know that the newborn needs to feel secure, wanted and loved to prosper. Body contact is vital to the infant.

Untold books have been published about correct child rearing. In our opinion there is NO ONE correct formula which is valid for all parents. We do know that trouble children are troubled children and hard to reprocess unless the parents are reprocessed. Children learn by example and by imitation. If we do not like what they have learned, we need to present a different example. What we offer, what we provide and what we expect are concepts which need to be revisited, probably revised. Parental self righteousness leaves the child out in the cold. Our "grown up" values and expectations simply make no sense to a child whose reasoning power is limited and whose emotional responses tend to infuriate the parent even more.

Whenever an occasion makes alarm bells ring, we want to take a deep breath and think about what is happening. When we master this approach it will reflect in our children. If your son comes to you crying and deeply disturbed, your best impulse is to give him a hug to make him feel better. Even better would be a follow up discussion about what or who caused his distress. If you do this consistently, the child will develop his own cognitive skills early on. Skills which will provide him with a problem solving capacity throughout his life.

Eric Berne, MD, in his book Games People Play provides a typical example of a parent child exchange. The parent is offering a hand of "I am only trying to help you". The response is likely to be "there is nothing you can do to help me" or "look how hard I'm trying". The result is a zero sum game. Had both tried to tackle the situation with more thought, and a focus on the problem, a better outcome would have resulted.

In recent years there has been a tendency of the psychiatric profession to provide an unending list of disorders noted in the young. What disturbs us is that most are declared as pathological, an illness, which in fact they may not be.

Autism is a disorder in children which hinders them from forming relationships and greatly limits their ability to communicate. They seemingly are unable to adapt to change and in general have trouble responding appropriately to their environment. The question must be asked if this is a genetic defense system or a failing of socialization. Often the afflicted children are bright, and some may be overly sensitive. In severe cases there may indeed be a neurological problem. We also suspect that painful experiences with fellow humans, perhaps from birth on, may lay the foundation for this problem at times. In milder cases a deeply introverted child may simply be unable to deal with heavily extraverted surroundings.

We must accept the fact that the child is not well adjusted. We debate that he is ill. It is a disturbance of the psychic structure. The child needs to be re-introduced gently to social life. Continuous support and security must accompany this effort. A contained environment with gradual exposure by trusted and reliable people may ultimately defuse this problem.

The opposite phenomenon is called hyperactive disorder. Here we are dealing with an aggressive child who is obstructionist and destructive. The child employs an extraverted mode of living out childhood pains. Making a mess in the world turns out to be an effective method of hiding internal psychic damage. Sitting still means feeling the pain.

Treatment, to start with, should focus on socializing the child. An educational effort making clear what is acceptable behavior and what is not. The benefits accruing to the child resulting from a change in his actions must be made clear. Trust must be established through ongoing support. Since they may well be reactions to childhood pain, autism and hyperactivity might best be addressed by seeking help from a therapist for the whole family to rework family interactions.

A brief comment about teenagers. The development stage when many of us regret having had children. In fact it is a period when communicating is extremely important. Our adult outlook now can be understood, even if it is not accepted. Our parental perspective must be broad enough to recognize that the teenager is trying to establish his own identity, which typically means that our views will be rejected. This is normal, though for most parents objectionable. It is also normal for teenagers to do "crazy" things occasionally, equally hard to digest by adults.

# Chapter 11

# Stressed Out

We all are. And there are a hundred books telling you what to do about it. Yet despite all this good advice, we are still stressed out. Our approach to this ongoing and worsening problem is different. We want to attack stress cognitively, we want us to manage it. For the benefit of all of us.

Some of us manage stress better than others. Our body produces chemicals which modulate our reaction to stressful events. There are natural non worriers, lucky ones who are genetically buffered against stress. Others have become hardened by experience. But most of us, even though not classifiable as sensitive, most of us suffer from being overstressed some, if not much of the time.

We propose that stress has two sides. One, we call the stressor, the cause of making us tense. The second side is the stressee, the victim of stress. Both ends of this interactive equation are subject to analysis and possible management and correction.

To a considerable extent stress is caused by global, societal and cultural conditions. The population on earth has grown exponentially with improved medicine and diet. As a result humanity is being ever more tightly squeezed into less and less private space. Some societies, like the Japanese, have established behavioral norms designed to cope with loss of personal space. But for billions on earth, privacy or finding some recreation in nature is not available. This, we know, causes stress.

Our societies used to be based on family units which were cohesive and geographically stable. Nowadays, particularly in America, which is space oriented, the family tends to beak up early with all members moving freely, often with great distances involved. The loss of familial support is another stressor.

Information and the resulting changes proceed at increasing speed and complexity. Day in day out we are subjected to thousands of efforts to leave an impression on us. In effect we are information aggression victims. To this we add the results of our own search for wanted information. The outcome is called overload, the result stress.

The world has become little more than a neighborhood sandbox. It has shrunk. And the inevitable squabbles which occur in the sandbox have become of concern to us, wherever they occur, wherever we live. It may be terrorism, it may be global warming or outsourcing of work. We have little, or no control over these issues which now cause stress. The Germans have a word to describe this frustrating condition, it is Weltschmerz.

Literally translated it means global pain and it includes a dose of self serving sentimentality.

When we Americans visit foreign countries we cannot help but notice that we stick out like the proverbial sore thumb. We seem too loud, too visible, too present. Generally we feel ok about sticking out, leaning on our self confidence. But even within our own society dissonance may occur should you be a very introverted individual living amidst a widely extraverted populace. Due to no fault of your own, may feel misplaced and stressed out.

The stressors we have listed above are beyond our external management capacity. We must deal with them within ourselves. There are many steps we can take, and they will be discussed later.

There have been attempts at ranking the severity and impact of various life events. Without a doubt the death of a loved one must rank at the top. Thereafter it is very much a matter of how we as individuals react. In order to get a handle on this diverse palette of trouble makers, we will briefly list the most common issues.

Family items rank at the top of the list. Marital conflicts are an everyday issue. Children get equal rating. Parents and in-laws can cause major stress. Tied to family life is the security of the household. Finances are a many faced dilemma. Who has control over money. Who earns what and who spends what. Who gets the blame for the lack of income. What to do when bills outweigh earning power. The list is long.

Work life is another heavy weight. Most of us spend more time at the workplace than awake at home. Conflicts with superiors and with co-workers threaten our self esteem and our security. Changing jobs or a change in position are looming dangers.

Our social entanglements can be stressful. We treasure our real friendships and need the support of whatever group we belong to. A rupture from, even what we experience as criticism from those we lean on, will cause stress.

We never have enough time to accomplish what we are supposed to do. Having to rush all day long, worse not getting done what was planned or expected, is bad news for our equanimity.

Our sexual activities are frequent issues brought to therapy. They do not lend themselves easily to sharing with our regular trouble-sharing partners. Capacity and performance have found a seemingly huge response in the current flood of ED medications. Mutuality has been a stressor of more recent times. A long list of drugs designed to enhance libido is awaiting FDA approval. In the meantime, what may be a natural drop in interest in sexual activity is perceived as a shortcoming causing stress.

Living conditions, housing and moving are frequent items brought to the table. Today a stunningly large percentage of 18 to 26 year olds still live at home. Here we have a sure sign of general stress in the making. Our ever upward mobility, and the resulting short term residence in any one house create multiple sources of unease.

Festivals like Christmas and major birthdays are supposed to be joyful events. In fact they are at best a mixed bag. Therapists' offices are crowded with distressed people during these times. This observation can be broadened to the extent that many positive events are highly stressful. Taking that long awaited vacation in Europe stands most of us on end. Getting married has all participants in full dress and deep stress.

This listing would not be complete if we did not mention "self caused" stress. The thoughts we ourselves generate, such as "I should", " I should not", "I must", "What if" are powerful stressors.

Our body sends us potent messages when we are stressed out. These are messages we should listen to. If we want to improve our health we must listen to them, but not fear them Recognizing our symptoms as warning signs, not as fatal flaws is the correct approach.. Typical symptoms we have observed include the following disturbances.

Muscle aches

Muscle cramps

High blood pressure

Rapid pulse

Asymmetric heartbeat

Back pain

Over eating, weight gain

Too much alcohol consumption

Headache

Excessive perspiration

Fatigue plus sleep disorder

Immune system disorders

Catching colds easily

Oral infections

Skin disorders

Inflamed tendons and nerves

And as should be expected, bedmates of stress come in the form of anxiety and depression.

Managing stress is made easier if we are able to pinpoint the source and impact when it occurs. And we literally mean right then and there. So much psychic trouble is the result of an event repressed at the moment we face it and are unable or unwilling to deal with it. Of course it is not always possible to resolve problematic issues on the spot. But making a mental note, if possible a written note, of the event will enable us to rethink the issue and make plans for its resolution. The key is keeping unresolved issues conscious, on the table so to speak.

A predominant number of stressors involve personal relationships.

We have discussed the negotiating, win-win approach to solving these situations. It is worth remembering that most personal connections are voluntary, meaning that we are not imprisoned by them. This specifically includes our employment. We are at our work station by consent. When we face a challenge, perhaps even a confrontation in a relationship, we must have sufficient assertiveness and self confidence on our end of the scale. Giving in, giving up or making a self sacrifice in order to preserve the connection will only result in further stress.

Our feelings are real and we can disclose them. We can say NO without having to feel guilty. Even complaining is appropriate as long as we state the issue from our perspective with "I" messages as opposed to "you" messages. And at all times we should be congruent. It is wrong to offer a warm smile when describing hurt feelings, or saying that something is a small problem, when in fact we are deeply disturbed by it.

Not only are adults stressors, but children can overload us just as much. Presumably we do have a stronger hand in this case, and we are able to set certain rules. Whenever possible such rules should make sense to both sides which requires some explaining and reasoning. Rules include limits, schedules and issues of shared responsibility. Before going to the mat, we should be sure that whatever calls for a discussion, is worth the investment. Sometimes just letting it go saves energy and mutual goodwill.

As stressees we can work through issues which bother us, and when necessary accept the unchangeable. This latter choice means we have to deal with and somehow digest something unpleasant life has dished out. A complex humanistic philosophy includes meditation, as proposed by Buddha, and it is a calming method of dealing with stress. Due to the current popularity of this way of living, we will attempt to present some of its key points....and problems.

Buddha focused on experience and drew the inevitable conclusion that life means suffering. In general his solution focuses on a change from what we have to who we are. An abandonment of material cravings and ego trips will help make life manageable This is a transfer from the sensual to the spiritual. Deliverance means no passion, no good luck, no bad luck, no possessive love, no hate.

Buddhism is non theistic, a non metaphysical point of view. Our individual experience is the criterion of our truth, and we as individuals are responsible for our acts.

Meditation in a quiet place permits us to let problems float away. It is Buddha's fourth truth leading to inner peace. Unnecessary suffering is lifted out and shed. The result is wisdom and spiritual insight. A state of being which unites both inner and outer worlds bringing with it a true knowledge

Carl Jung who studied Buddhism at length saw its value. At the same time he felt that we westerners would be hindered by our intellectual approach finding the required experiential approach un-natural. He went so far as to accuse many western followers of Buddha as pitiable imitators. He did conclude that spirit is a higher plane than intellect and that Buddhism can bring about a unity of personality. Meditation, he added, is a light which enters on its own. Let it happen, let go of yourself and a harmony and a unity of life will appear.

Yoga is another aspect of combining body and psyche. Both philosophies meet natural resistance from our ingrained morals, intellectualism and religious underpinnings. Our final recommendation is that you give yoga and meditation a try. You may never reach spiritual unity or see the light, but you may gain from solitude and time to reflect in a moment of peace on your situation and problems.

A down to earth method of containing stress are time and task management. We all must admit to ourselves that we forget. The solution, making lists of what needs to be done and when. Should we fail with an assignment, presto, it can go on the next day's schedule. Remembering is a major stressor, get rid of it and let one of those small digital devices carry the burden, or in our case, keep a pad of paper handy, and use it on a daily basis.

Schedules open the door to additional review. Can we simplify our lives and simply delete certain activities, or share the task with others. Perhaps we can delegate them altogether and let others perform the task. It is a matter of self discipline to set limits on ourselves. It is a temptation to yield to the shortcut of doing it yourself rather than asking others to cooperate and help.

For many, exercise has proven to be a stress release. Our body produces chemicals during workouts which boost our morale and spirit. Reducing muscle tension via exercises has similar results. This calls for some discipline, not easy to muster when stress has worn us down.

The abolition of stress is not a realistic objective. We want to reduce its impact through managing it issue by issue. A certain amount of temporary recovery can be gained through recreation, by using our sense of humor and perhaps laughing the whole problem off.

Seeking and getting help is not a sign of weakness. All too often when the stressor is a person, this very focal point of stress will turn out to provide the help we needed. Friends, family and co-workers can turn into freebee problem solvers for us. We will revisit this topic in a later chapter in greater detail.

# Chapter 12

# Trauma

The word trauma has come to be generally used for almost any unpleasant event. Having a root canal cleared out, being called into the boss's office, waiting for the results of a cat scan, all merit the description of trauma in our conversation today. In medicine the word is used to identify a physical injury. We prefer to limit the use of the word trauma to a severe, even cataclysmic psychic injury.

Otto Rank considered our birth as the original trauma in life. Being forcefully expelled from the warmth and comfort of the womb, he claimed, inflicted a deep and lasting injury on all of us. Freud (1893) suggested that it is "like a foreign body" in us.

Traumatic experiences can occur throughout our lives. The older we get, the more reasoning we can apply to what happens to us, the better we cope with dramatic events. And it is to be expected that some of us are sturdier when faced with a calamity than others. What is evident however, is that traumatic events experienced in infancy and childhood are very likely to leave not only a scar, but permanent psychological damage.

Many events can be perceived as catastrophic. Abuse can be physical and invasive, or more subtle in the form of neglect or abandonment. Even a relatively minor interruption of parental contact may leave a lasting impact. Here children become the object and are used by adults to vent their own frustrations or fulfill their own needs. Traumatic events overwhelm children emotionally. From a perceived loss of love to humiliation and violence, a feeling of deep helplessness results. Children cannot master or discharge these injuries which, as a result, are repressed into the unconscious. There they fester and express themselves as somatic reactions, complexes, neuroses and even psychotic breakdown.

Undigested trauma has been given its own name: post traumatic stress syndrome. World War One brought this disorder to light when soldiers broke down from "shell shock". Later conflicts created a new name for the same reaction to battle trauma, it became "battle fatigue". In this case adults broke down, became dysfunctional due to their inability to cope with extreme stress. So it is not just a childhood problem, but one any one of us may succumb to, at any time. Survivors of bad accidents in cars or planes are typical examples.

Victims of post traumatic stress disorder tend to re-experience the event in dreams, painful memories and flashbacks of the actual event. Contrary reactions may be common, such as avoidance of any reminder of the cause of the trauma. General numbness helps dull the impact of the initial experience. These are natural defenses designed to ward off having to relive the trauma.

Permanent physiological changes and serious illness may be the result of trauma. Both are stark reminders that body and mind are one.

Children lack the capacity to manage trauma. The loss of security or love will have them seeking opportunities to re-create what they lost. Failing in this effort, they will suffer from nightmares, restlessness and may develop phobias or fears related to the original traumatic event.

The unfortunate victims of post traumatic stress tend to be hypervigilant, always on guard ready to defend themselves against a perceived threat. Often they lose the ability to distinguish between real danger, or perceived threats, in fact harmless events. As a result they tend to be in a near constant state of arousal. Strange sounds, smells, or being touched can set them off into a state of deep anxiety. This being an unconscious reaction designed to protect them from what occurred during the original injury.

Helping victims of trauma calls for professional intervention. Therapy involves the re-discovery of the original event. With the help of the therapist the victim will gradually become aware of the original feelings and able to deal with them. Facing the wound will slowly lead to living with it. A competent therapist will help by replacing good experiences for the bad ones implanted by the trauma.

There is an exception to this approach. When the initial trauma is perceived as utterly hideous, overwhelmingly devastating, it may well be that the victim cannot afford to rediscover it. To do so might re-traumatize the victim, making the pain and suffering even worse. The victim may well give signs that re-opening the door must be avoided.

## Chapter 13

# Getting Help

There is more than confusion, but outright misperception about the training, and qualification of therapists. Again and again we have suggested that "talking things out" is not only palliative, but is a proven way of resolving problematic issues. There are times when the pain is too intense, the trouble too complex, and you seek help from a therapist. In many circles there remains a stigma attached to psychological problems and problem solving. "Tough it out", "you can handle it" is bad advice handed out by those who consider emotional problems "abnormal".

There is no need for you to fly blind. Your physician my give you a good lead. Many communities have social service centers offering counseling. A friend or a family member may have a recommendation, so may your spiritual adviser. It is well worth your time to check out who is who in your therapist community.

A psychiatrist is an MD, a qualified physician with a specialty in psychology. Our review of curricula of medical schools tends to indicate that not all of them require great exposure to actual therapy. As physicians, psychiatrists are qualified to prescribe medication. We strongly feel that medication is appropriate and useful in a crisis, or as a bridge during therapy. Medication does not solve problems, it covers up symptoms.

A psychologist is a graduate with a degree in psychology. The top level is a PhD, a doctor of philosophy degree in this specialty. Individuals holding this certification have been broadly exposed to their profession. They have limited training in the physiological aspects of health care.

A psychoanalyst may lean on several academic specialties and degrees. Both MDs and PhDs may have gone through the lengthy training required to become an analyst. Even holders of certain masters degrees have been admitted to analytical training. Training proper is conducted by Jungian and Freudian Institutes and others in a limited number of urban areas. The educational process is lengthy and intensive and therapy oriented.

MSW is a masters degree awarded in social work schools at universities. Licensed clinical social workers (LCSW) have had considerable training in both social work and psychological therapy.

All of the above professionals are licensed according to national accreditation bodies or by the states in which they practice.

There are many others working under the umbrella of a number of classifications, such as counselor, diplomate or simply therapist.

You should find the person in whom you have confidence and with whom you are at ease and comfortable. We have mentioned informal channels such as friends and family members several times. With them, a latent danger lies in the possibility of overloading them with your troubles. This, in turn, could cause a rupture in your relationship.

It may be difficult for you to decide if and when you may want to consult a professional therapist. If you chose this path, you will find that after some actual exposure you may find it easier to determine how deeply you need or want to explore your psyche.

The training of the therapist has much to do with the intensity and depth of the work you can do with him. It is our firm view that the better qualified therapist has done much work on his own psyche, and the more the better. We all have issues which would benefit from additional exploration. The cleaner the plate which your therapist brings to the table, the better for you. His objectivity is essential to YOUR work with YOUR issues.

Counselors may offer you guidance. A good therapist will let you discover who you really are, not who you should be. Living with the real true you is your best way to inner peace.

## Chapter 14

# Healing

Our bodies and our minds tend toward stasis. We are constructed to maintain our health. Sickness and pain are abnormal and, automatically, our whole self goes to work to make repairs. Healing is not a process imposed on us. WE must provide the power and support to get healed. A physician and a therapist can help us, but it is up to us to do the job.

This chapter is long. We will propose a number of ways and methods to help you help yourself. Intentionally we have not assigned priorities or a weighting to this array of health builders. We have found that our individuality lays the foundation for the right choices.

We do urge you to go through this list again and again, until you have found the right way, or combination of ways for you.

**Diagnosis.** Knowing and understanding what ails us is a critical step to recovery. We have offered a number of tools and methods designed to help the reader identify and rectify psychological troubles. This process starts with the question: "what's wrong?" As we indicated, psychosomatic illness is a frequent fellow traveler of emotional disorder. Seeing your primary health care provider will generally provide a handle which lets you evaluate the possible seriousness of the symptoms.

Medical science has provided physicians with a vast array of diagnostic tools. Physicians have confided in us that diagnosis, despite scientific progress, is still somewhat of a guessing game. The biggest problem is the patient who is unable or unwilling to fully describe both the emotional and physiological components of the perceived trouble. Reticent patients may respond more freely if they are approached with a more neutral question like: "what's going on with you?"

An even bigger difficulty, as we see it, are physicians themselves. The car mechanic approach toward illness is still a prevailing attitude. The mechanic does his job when he fixes the squeak in the rear springs. He overlooks the fact that the springs have rusted through and need replacing. This means that all too many physicians who find a physiological symptom will make every effort to fix that symptom, disregarding that other, possibly psychological aspects of the person may be in dire need of an overhaul.

Two current studies illustrate this dilemma. Researchers at the University of California in San Francisco (Epel and Blackburn) have found that stress ages us prematurely. They found that damage at the basic

DNA level becomes a permanent injury caused by our inability to manage stress. The cause: psychological, the result: physiological damage.

Another bit of research was concurrently published in the Journal of Neuroscience (Apkarian). In this study the researchers concluded that persistent back pain caused a shrinkage of the gray matter in the brain. This shrinkage was evaluated as the equivalent of a loss due to 10 to 20 years of normal aging.

In our view this research has put the cart before the horse. It is more likely that the psychological disturbance came first. It caused the back pain and the shrinkage of brain cells due to stress.

The conclusion to be drawn is that it is up to you to help the physician, if called upon, to diagnose your situation from all human perspectives. It is up to you to seek second opinions and YOU are in charge of working out a solution with the advice of a professional.

Accept Psychosomatic Symptoms for what they are. It is your mind sending out a warning. A problem wants to be recognized, wants to be heard.

**Treasure the Moment.** It is not only stress we meet face to face all day long. Little treasures, little gifts are equally abundant. Inhale the smell of the freshly brewed coffee in the morning. Savor it. Sooner or later, someone will give you a big smile. Absorb it all the way to your inner depths. Someone approves of you. Great. Return this gesture and put your feelings into it. Give. Perhaps while driving to work, someone yields and lets you sneak in. Wave a big thank you to this road angel. You'll both feel better.

**Try and notice the simple beauty offered everywhere.** Look at the flowers in the vase or in the garden. The clouds above, with the sun setting, a play of purples, pinks and grays. Take it in, it will never be the same again.

**Give your partner an unexpected hug.** Scratch your dog's ears and catch the grateful look of appreciation. We can be observers, we can initiate and we can receive little chips of beauty all day long. We must be conscious of these gifts, and like money in the savings account, we build up a pile of assets which will defend us when stress hits. The human tendency to overlook the positive and react to the negative is self defeating. It is up to you to start this savings account right now.

**Take care of Yourself....first.** We all have heard the instruction of the flight attendant telling us to put the oxygen mask on our face first, and only then put it on others flying with us. Our lives are filled with relationships where we bear responsibility. We will do the best job when we are in good shape, when we have taken care of ourselves.

**Spoil Yourself, at least a little.** So, for many of us, our ancestors were puritans. Forget it. They just lacked the opportunity to have some fun. Get the massage, order the expensive menu item, buy that pair of shoes or that fancy electronic gizmo. Get away by yourself. Close the door, relish the bit of privacy, the silence of being with and within yourself.

**Exercise.** It is a proven fact that muscle and tendon pains, those tension cramps are relieved by motion. Stress and tension make us clench our muscles which squeezes the blood out of them. This loss of blood means less oxygen for the muscles which makes them painful. Thus pain in muscles, tendons and ligaments can very likely be the result of too little oxygen in those tissues. Improving blood flow to these areas through exercise, even simple motion, is likely to reduce discomfort.

Depression is lightened by regular exercise. Some get an actual high from it. Regular exercise requires self control, mastering the impulse to sit and turn on he TV. Your health and your longevity are influenced by your physical activity and condition.

There are groups and exercise outfits where you will be encouraged by others to come along and stay with it. Professional exercise experts vary in what you "should" do. What feels right to you? Is it 30 minutes of Jazzercise or an hour of aerobics. You can even be casual about it. Walk up the two flights of stairs instead of taking the elevator. Walk to work, or to bus station two stops down. 30 minutes a day of using your body in activity is good for you. Even pushing a vacuum counts. All of it is better than doing nothing. Go to it.

**Look for and get Reassurance.** We never outgrow the need to be told that we are ok. A physician friend of ours told us that if you regularly leave your doctor's office feeling worse than you did when you came in, the doctor is in the wrong field. He should have become a pathologist or an anesthesiologist.

It is totally correct to ask for reassurance. "Is that the way you wanted it done?" "Does it bother you that I am telling you this?" "You are sure this discoloration on my skin is nothing bad?" You are not fishing for a compliment, you want to, and need to know that things are in order, meaning you are.

**Make sure you belong.** Our initial support group was, and still may be our family. Homo Sapiens is a social animal. Even introverts need human contact for relatedness and connection. Being with others gives us comfort and the feeling of collective safety.

As we age our relations extend to friends, neighbors and co-workers. Common interests let us join others in associations, clubs, societies and parties. It is confirming and self validating to be with those who share our points of view.

Loneliness is surprisingly common in our overcrowded world. The lonely may be victims of rejection and lack the courage to try again. The hurt of being turned away is uniquely painful and destructive. The lonely tend to get morose; joining a group is the easiest way to try to re-enter into relationships. The diversity of groups encourages acceptance.

As we age our search for connectedness extends in social and historic dimensions. We relate and connect the past, the present and the future. We try to discover where we came from, who our ancestors were and what they did. We undertake efforts which tie us into history, something relevant and meaningful.

Making a connection with life around us, with nature, is a valid search. Many look beyond, into the universe to see where we fit in. Religion can be another bond which connects us to an ultimate power.

**Manage your Finances.** One of the most common and ordinary causes of distress and conflict is money. Not only the lack of same, but the question of who spends how much and on what. The source of trouble we encounter most frequently is secrecy. One of the partners in a relationship conceals financial activities. This relates to both spending and saving. Mutual disclosure and joint decision making about money matters are essential to keeping peace in close relationships.

Managing finances together includes insurance policies and retirement schemes. We Americans as a society are poor savers. We love to spend and delayed gratification is a myth. Money troubles for those near or at retirement age have become a fast growing source of relationship conflict. Untold times we have heard the plaintiff comment: "we never had time to talk about it."

**Ask for Advice.** It is no joke that men don't ask for directions, because it is denigrating, a loss of stature. The undeniable fact is, however, that there are those who have information we may need. Many of us, perhaps most of us have mastered basic computer skills. The internet has become a treasure trove of information. If not free, it is inexpensive. Add to this vast source the people in your circle who may offer opinions about your question. Your objective is to create a wider selection of choices from which you can select those suitable to you.

**Sharing.** An ancient, and still true proverb has it that any pleasure shared is a pleasure doubled, and that any sorrow shared is a sorrow cut in half. Our language has its own idiom for this activity. It is bending someone's ear. Another one is dumping on people. The opposite idiom is sitting on an experience with an implied connotation that sitting on it is not good for you. And that is a basic fact. In our view the entire process of therapy involves letting loose what you were sitting on.

Sharing calls for some judgment. There are indeed good listeners, but "talking their heads off" will lose you friends. Probably we all have encountered strangers who for some reason have felt free to tell us intricate and personal stories. Putting impact-full experiences into words takes them out of our minds and out into the open. Sharing is a release, and unless overdone, good for us. The discovery that there are others who are struggling with problems, that we are not alone, is very comforting.

**See the Funny side of it.** Even tragic events bring out what is called gallows humor. If we can laugh at the devil, he shrivels up. Humor brings a different dimension to what otherwise is troubling.

We gravitate to people who have an easy smile and open laugh. Join them, learn from them and the burden will get lighter.

**Talk to Yourself, out loud if possible.** We all agree that our heads are crammed full of stuff. Talking out loud ventilates some of the material into the open, for you to hear, for you to react to. Letting off steam describes the process.

Even more important is talking to yourself with an instructional component. When anxiety hits, telling yourself: "It is ok. I am ok" over and over again will help you overcome negative emotions. Those who suffer from psychosomatic illnesses have succeeded by yelling at themselves when a pain recurs. Coupled with high intensity, the order given to our mind to "quit it", has been successful in the prevention of somatic outbursts.

**Reality Check.**  Throughout these pages we have encouraged you to hold emotions in check. Out of control, they overpower us and our perception of reality gets warped. This is not to be construed as  a denial of feelings, but a wake-up call to thinking, to cognitive appraisal of any situation.

Under pressure our imagination has the ability to present possible future outcomes which are way beyond normal expectancy. When we envision catastrophes, it is time to shout "hold the horses" at ourselves. It is time to pull out our little notepad and write down all possible outcomes and next to them  assign to each a key as to the probability of its occurrence; ranging from zero with very unlikely, to 10, most likely. A question mark behind an outcome means that you need to gather more facts to make an evaluation. This simple process will take the steam out of the situation.

Reality checking is equally valid for memories. We remember what we want to remember. Additionally we add our own flavor and emotions to what happened. Reality tends to get dimmer and ever more infused with the way we want to recall an event. Our challenge is simple. Every recall is an opportunity to reframe our memory. We can defuse excessive emotions often tied to past events.

**Animal Friends.** Call them pets, call them companions, in plain language, they are our friends, perhaps our best friends. From wet fish to slithery snakes and warm and fuzzy dogs to independent cats to horses and hamsters. Add rats and mice and a vast array of birds. All of them are company. We talk to them and some of them talk back, with voices, with feelings, with actions.

We share our homes, our space and our strained budgets with our companions. They, in turn, accept us, try to please us, entertain us and, in their way, love us back. Animals take us out of ourselves and into their world. It is easy for us to get preoccupied with our own situation. Entering and sharing another life offers relief. If these features are appealing to you, and you have never had an animal friend, give it a try, it is a good experience.

Cruelty to animals is an every day occurrence. We all have had to "straighten out" our dog when he dragged the roast from the kitchen table. But using an animal as an outlet for our frustrations is wrong and criminal. People who succumb to committing animal violence are sick and need professional help.

**Get Touched.** An essential part of an infant's feeling of security is body contact. After the lengthy residency in a cozy womb, being tossed into a cold blanket is a shock. Pictures of mothers in Africa and South America with their babies bundled on their backs or in front give evidence of what must be natural. Providing ongoing body contact with the mother, or a mother personality offers security to an infant.

As we grow up and mature, we are encouraged to outgrow a number of comforts of childhood. Thumb sucking, holding on to the slick edge of our blanket and insisting that Teddy sleep with us may have to yield to being an adult. But body contact must not be discarded.

Holding hands with one you care for and cuddling up with your partner are high potency comfort pills. Lacking freebee human comfort, spend some money and get a massage. It can be soothing and set you up for the day.

In these times when trial lawyers seem to rule the roost, casual and well intended touching to offer support at work, even in social life may be misunderstood, perhaps intentionally. So touch, but only those you know are touchable.

**Turn Tasks into Routines.** A task is a job which requires planning, allocating resources, meaning time and effort and getting it done. Routines are tasks which we perform on a regular and repetitive basis. This eliminates the planning process altogether and time and effort can be streamlined because we get more and more efficient at performing routines. We gain and grow a sense of power via the efficacy when what we must do, we do well and efficiently.

**Put on a Happy Face.** Selling yourself on handing out a smile instead of a frown, pays off. We are speaking of your view of your own situation, not necessarily how you address the outside world. It is a fact that we can recondition our automatic reactions to life. Whenever you feel like expelling a deep sigh and sense that nothing good lies ahead, stop and restart the engine. What is ahead may be a challenge, something for you to master. Taking it on with spirit will give you a leg up on overcoming it. More important, you will feel good about doing it, and about YOURSELF.

**Be Proactive.** The opposite of this approach is to react. Reacting has us on our heels, possibly even in a defensive mode. Some of us are naturally passive. Then you let it happen to you, whatever it may be. Taking charge, directing the course of your inner life will have positive results. It will empower you and enhance the outcome of your outer life. This calls for some assertiveness, not easy for the shy and introverted. But tooting your own horn places the most qualified advocate of your assets in front.

**Alternative Medicine.** Traditionalists consider psychology alternative medicine. We have made the point that mind and body are ONE. Treating one without the other is a half done job. However most of us subscribe to additional methods to maintain our health, and it is our view that whatever improves your state, is worth a good try.

Dietary supplements are an everyday effort we undertake to boost our health. Vitamins, minerals and joint maintenance products are standard additions to our diet. Add to this herbal teas and the entire array of Chinese herbal medicines. Homeopathy, the treatment of illness with tiny herbal portions is blooming, and successful for many patients.

Acupuncture, yoga and meditation are beneficial imports from Asia. Tai Chi, the controlled slow body motion exercise has benefited many. Hypnosis has been of help in the discovery of deeply seated memories, as it has been used to ease compulsive behavior.

**Time Out.** Get away from it. We Americans are a notoriously over worked society. This will take a toll. When locked in, we have a tendency to stay locked in. Break the chain. Take a vacation. For your own good, take some earned sick leave. When relationships are strained, give them some slack. Rather than digging ever deeper, take a break. Some distance and some time may be just what is needed for repair.

**Give a little Love.** This can be one of our best investments. Love usually begets love. Expand this concept to benefiting others. Caring for those in need empowers us. Doing good, does us good, makes us feel good.

**Eat and Sleep Well.** Grandmother suggested that if you sleep badly, eat more. This well meant advice seems to have become a national edict. Proper eating habits are the topic of books and the stern advice of the Surgeon General. Over-eating is comforting. If you cherish your looks and your health, find love and support in other sources than a gallon of ice cream.

**Get in Touch with your True Feelings.** Love thy neighbor and your parents are religious imperatives.

Morals and religious teachings may put us at odds with ourselves. Complainers are diminished as whiners. In our view well being depends on getting in touch and expressing your true feelings. The truth may be ugly and hurtful and needs to be handled thoughtfully with others. But it will put you on your feet, "set you free".

## Chapter 15

# Hope, Faith and Expectation

At first glance these three words look simple and are part of everyday casual conversation. But when we started to debate their meaning, we realized their complexity.

We hope for a wish to come true. It is a future oriented concept. We hope for change. The flag of hope hangs limply on the pole until a wind from a greater power straightens it.

Faith is beyond reason, it is spiritual. It does not rely on knowledge or facts. Trust is experiential, faith is ephemeral, translucent. Its opponent is doubt. Doubt springs from reason.

Hope and faith, when combined lead us to positive expectation. This is a winning combination without rational underpinnings. It is not an escape for the weak, dumb or uneducated, but a reality. It is a solution, not a rope from which we dangle, but a foundation. Then we do not need to know the future and can let happen what will happen.

Science and the scientific method of revalidating a proven formula are seen by many as the final reality. We propose that this is the reality of our world, and these facts may not be universally applicable. Looking into the sky we struggle with the nearly incomprehensible phenomenon of eternity and infinity. Current cosmology suggests that our universe is but one bubble among many others. Our science therefore is ultimately based on faith that "our rules" are valid elsewhere.

An interesting intersection of science and spirituality occurred in a number of supervised experiments reported in numerous articles in medical journals. We have mentioned that the healing power of prayer and faith were proven with patients who were the subject of the spiritual intervention. The results were demonstrable improvement or recovery. This occurred even when they did not know they were being prayed for.

Faith, the belief in something greater than yourself, is personal. It is the ultimate expression of individuality. For many it is based on God, for others on nature, or as one of our colleagues stated, the Big Something. Faith permits us to let go of controlling what we cannot control. Faith permits us to turn over anxious worrying to a designated worrier. Faith makes fate a supervised commodity.

As we age we increasingly feel that our lives should have meaning. Why are we here, what have we accomplished, are nagging questions. For many of us the nature of our acquisitive society has failed to provide us with purpose and happiness. In our view this meaning

we seek is not an issue of a purposeful search, but of experience. If and when we feel that our life is rich and rewarding, we are on the right track. If not, it is time for change, might this be physical, emotional or spiritual. Our culture is basically one where we feel we have some handle on our fortune. Fate, Karma or other ways describing a predetermined path of life are not what western societies perceive as the meaning of life.

Death is a part of life. It is the ultimate unknown. Near death experiences have been reported, as have communications between the dead and the living via a medium. Despite these events, death means the loss of any control, the loss of consciousness and of our physical being. The world's major religions, Christianity, Islam, Judaism and Hinduism, all assure us of an after life. This calls for the ultimate embracing of faith. It is the acceptance of every ending being the beginning of something new. This concept may well be applied to both weddings and funerals.

In conclusion we want to quote from a speech delivered by the Honorable Joanne Parrilli of the California Court of Appeal to the Saint Thomas More Society at Santa Clara University.

"Thomas More believed that people had a religious consciousness, an intuition that existed above reason, but harmonized with it. As a Christian More held that the church with its centuries of tradition and hosts of Saints was a natural development of the fundamental religious consciousness in all human beings."

Justice Parilli's closing comments focused on the last letter written by Thomas More from the Tower, the day before his execution.

"The letter focuses only on love and only on others, their virtues, their well-being, his hopes and blessings for them. And I imagine on our own deathbeds we won't be thinking about how the bishops behaved in the 21st century. If we're lucky, we'll be like Thomas More, ready to leave this earth and be with God and our loved ones again some day, confident that we made all the important choices that we faced with God and them in mind."

## Chapter 16

# Two Case Histories

We intentionally limited the number of case histories in our discussion because we think that YOU are the focus. Yet we think you are also entitled to know something about us. Like you, we are no more and no less than human. Our lives have not been easy, and we both have spent many hours trying to work out OUR problems.

There are two stories to follow. One about Klaus and his father experience. Freud said in 1930: I cannot think of any need in childhood as strong as the need for a father's protection.

**My Fathers.**

Our first dog was named Juno, as were all four who followed her. Juno five, another German Shepherd is still a family member today. But Juno one deserves special mention. I bought her from San Francisco's leading pet shop on Maiden Lane. Considering we both were still university students, the purchase was not only financially irresponsible, but amounted to having a baby requiring daycare while we were in class.

Juno, though a papered purebred was no show dog. She was small, even scrawny and one of her ears never stood up. But she was what Lynda wanted, something furry to hug and love.

Even more prematurely we decided to build our own home in Marin County, our stressed money flow now comatose. As Juno once again came in heat, we made a bold financial decision: Let's breed her. In the paper we saw that others were selling German Shepherd puppies for between one and two hundred dollars in the mid 1950s. Multiply that by six, maybe seven puppies and we had money to spend on overdue bills.

In no time flat, a breeder in Santa Rosa was found and Lynda made a date to consummate this profitable relationship, even though the process required another hundred in advance. But, the breeder promised, if it did not take, we would get a second try for free.

When I returned from work on the wedding day, I found Lynda somewhat humbled and shaken. The entire process deeply embarrassing for her. But it was done and according to the breeder, "a good take". During the remainder of the week a host of horny male dogs continued to hang around our house and all we did was shoo them away from the front door. Juno did her routines which involved roaming the neighboring fields and streets and she returned looking messy and harassed.

On the blessed day Juno delivered eight squealing little worms all on her own. We were jubilant. We had struck gold. After two months we ran an ad advertising our cash crop. This despite the inevitable fact that the puppies lacked the clean appearance of long nosed German Shepherds. Worse, their coloring was from jet black to deep gray, in no relation to either Juno or pop. Their ears floppy and their snouts bulky. Prospective buyers were assured that the pups would grow out of these features and in support we proudly handed out papers listing the distinguished purebred heritage of the little dogs. In no time flat we sold out, leaving but one for us to keep. As Judy, her name, grew up, she left no doubt as to her fatherhood. It had to have been a black Labrador.

To our surprise, only one customer called to complain. He wanted his money back. We offered to do so with the condition that he had to return the dog. We never heard from him again. When we called our breeder he told us that dogs "can take" from any number of males. Nothing like human beings where one male when done, shuts the door to further fertility. "Now he tells us" was Lynda's laconic reaction.

This experience does little to help explain the title of this story. As a human being, I had but one biological father. In fact, like our puppies, I had several fathers. My real father was Kurt Heinrich Schmidt, a stern task master, in turn the son of an even sterner father, a world famous surgeon. Perhaps it was in jest that my father claimed to have addressed his dad as "Herr Vater", Mister Father.

My specific memories relating to my own father are few, though vivid. Whenever he returned from work he would come into my room and issue the terse command to "make order". In fact, I was not only messy, but a slacker, un-athletic and ran to my mother whenever my brother, who was my father's true son, would get the best of me.

When I was little my father would take delight in tossing me into the air and....catch me. This airborne experience frightened me to the bone, indicating that my essential trust in dad was lacking. As the years went by my father avoided me, at least it seemed that way. Only two positive conversations he had with me come to mind. One related to his war experience in the naval battle at "Skagerak" (Jutland) when he served as an officer in WWI on the battle cruiser Seydlitz. His ship was turned into scrap metal, but he survived and won the Iron Cross for bravery. As he perceived me, bravery was not one of my assets. And he was right.

The second occasion took place in 1943 when his factories produced time fuses for the German army. He was called to the missile test site at Peenemuende to witness the performance of his products. To my utter surprise, even consternation, he invited me come along as his "Begleiter", the chap who carries his briefcase and documents. I was jubilant somehow feeling that this invitation was an expression of  trust and perhaps affection. Hours before our departure the whole affair was cancelled, Peenemuende having been bombed by the Allies and severely damaged.

As the war dragged on, my father increasingly and openly turned against Hitler. During a meeting with top officials he urged that Germany should seek an immediate cease fire since the war was lost. This  statement was the equivalent of  defeatism and made him subject to incarceration and death. After receiving a last minute warning from a local Gestapo chief, my parents decided to try and escape to Switzerland, where my paternal grandparents lived.

The last time I saw my father he was in tears having been refused asylum in Switzerland. To see my father cry broke my heart. It wiped out all the negative feelings, even hatred, I had built up over the years.

The Swiss took me in. My relatives found me as undigestable as my father had. I was offered the option of checking into a boarding school or interviewing with a mixed Swiss-American family, which considered taking me in for a limited time. They did. Carl Briner, head of household and a successful insurance executive became my second father. He turned out to be non critical, outright supportive. A quiet man with a subtle sense of humor. The Briners were not a clustered family, everyone tended to go their own way. Despite this seeming lack of cohesion, I felt at home and protected.

While living with them, I learned that my parents and my brother had been executed by the Gestapo. At age 14 I became an orphan. This event was not totally unexpected, yet I was unable to absorb what had happened. I cannot recall the feelings which made me decide to join my family in death via a hunger strike. After two or maybe three days of refusing to eat, Carl joined me at the breakfast table one morning, something he had never done before. A man of few words, he sat me down and said: "I know what you are trying to do. I cannot blame you, but let me assure you that what you are doing is wrong. Your family wants you to live, not die. So let's have a good breakfast together". We did.

Carl's acceptance facilitated my integration into Swiss society. At his urging I learned the local dialect and soon became indistinguishable from my school mates and the citizenry in general. After years of bitter war style and Nazi dominated living, The Briners opened the door to "the good life" for me. As a part of putting real legs under me, Carl introduced me into his athletic club, the Grasshopper Club of Zurich, specifically its rowing section. During all of my years in Switzerland I rowed with a passion, even winning a decent assortment of medals.

Before I decided to make America my home, Carl once again stood by me. He offered to put me through a Swiss university and get me started on a career of my choice. What more could I have asked from my real father?

My father had two brothers, Werner and the much younger Eberhard, nicknamed Hax. In the latter stages of the war Hax spent much time in our house. He had been given the vainglorious assignment of producing 1000 jet fighters per month in tunnels and caves spread throughout our province. His direct boss was one of the true monsters of Nazism, a man named Sauckel, later to be hanged after the Nuremberg trials. Throughout the ordeal of trying to gather manpower, tools and raw materials to fulfill his assignment, Hax never faltered. His incredible sense of humor rose above the impossible task. I recall one evening when he dropped in, my father asked him how it was going. With true gallows humor Hax responded that he had two screw drivers, four hammers, 100 party officials and 2000 Russian prisoners, all of them standing around six kettles in which a constant stew of boiled potatoes was brewing. And there he stood among them all reading an order from Sauckel that production was to begin the next day, or all would be shot on the spot.

Hax loved to laugh, loved making light of severe situations and making fun of all other people, often including himself. He was the only adult in that time who took me seriously. After my parents went to bed, he and I played chess into the late hours of the night. He always beat me, but never ceased giving me constructive advice. I idolized him.

Some years later Hax began a new life in Switzerland. His flat was not far from where I lived with the Briners. Without neglecting his own three sons, he took me under his wings too. Together we completed tortuous ski treks, like the Haute Route. He had lost one of his eyes in an early skiing accident and much to my amusement, every night his glass eye was deposited in a water glass, as he noted, to watch over us.

Having lost his wife to Nazi executioners, Hax included me in his deliberations about the marriage potential of his current lady friends. To be treated as a trustworthy adult became an essential part of my growing up experience. "After all you are my younger brother" he told me.

We stayed connected and saw each other annually. His advice throughout these many years was essential to my own success. After his retirement as CEO of a large Swiss corporation I was able to keep him in the flow of activity by garnering for him the position of visiting professor at my university. At the time we lived in a Victorian house in the Mission district of San Francisco.

To accommodate him we provided a small guest room with his own bath. After a week of trying to fit his six foot four frame into these quarters, he politely excused himself on the grounds that he was too old to live in a "ship's cabin".

Going back many years another father deserves mention and credit. My arrival in the USA was no haphazard event. Mary Briner, the American part of my Swiss parental figures, was a Jungian analyst. She paved my way via an introduction to an analyst colleague in the San Francisco Bay Area. His name Joseph B. Wheelwright. Since my planned studies were aimed at agriculture I had, what is best described as an internship with George Wheelwright, brother of this analyst. My initial home was on his ranch, where I was to sharpen my teeth doing "chores". Before heading for this Marin County cattle operation, known as Green Gulch Ranch, I was invited to spend a few days with Jo Wheelwright and his wife Jane. These days made the entry into the country of my future a breeze.

Jo was the same size as I, an uncomfortable six foot six. He spoke with an impeccable British accent and found something amusing about everyone he talked about. He was warm and welcoming. Three distinct memories from these days remain ingrained. Jo loved talking about his practice and his patients. Even though none of them meant anything to me, his commentary was ever so different from what I heard at the Briners. There, when other professionals came for a meal, the tone of the discussion seemed theoretical and abstract to me. I could not comprehend what these head games had to do with peoples' problems. Jo, on the other hand, talked about down to earth matters and situations and what might be done to help resolve them for his patients.

My interest in agriculture was probably a bit naïve. A deep seated distrust of people seemed to find a harmless resolution by dealing with animals or crops. Jo immediately sensed that this so called interest was more an escape rather than my destiny and future. Following this insight he jokingly suggested that I would probably find cows a bit boring on a day in day out basis and to compensate, I was invited to spend my weekends in his house. While doing this, he mused, I might meet his daughter Lynda, who also came home from the university over Saturday night. He thought I might like her. He was correct on all counts.

The third moment occurred just before Christmas 1949. The Wheelwrights had apparently decided to spend the holidays in the Santa Barbara area on the Hollister ranch with the parents of Jane Wheelwright. Jo took me aside and apologized sincerely that I was excluded and that he was truly sorry about this. This deep and obvious caring for me and my feelings was unforgettable.

As Lynda and I appeared to move ever closer to a permanent relationship, Jo gave us his wholehearted support. Even when he and I developed issues on which we not only differed, but loudly disagreed, he never rejected me. Our frequent meals with them, once we were married, were always a highlight, though frequently interrupted by patient calls. Usually, after Jo had been listening for a quarter hour, Jane would scream at the top of her lungs: "Jo, the dinner is getting cold." As a matter of fact his dinners were usually cold when he finally started to dig in. His carving of the chicken, leg of lamb, or beef roast was interminably slow and studded with wisecracks and ham acting. Then ensued a wine opening, decanting and tasting ceremony, all ending with his meal stiff and cold.

Jo had a keen sense of what I needed to do to understand America and Americans . As I entered Cal, I was invited to join one of the fraternities. When I discussed the pros and cons of such a commitment, Jo urged me in the strongest terms to join up, which I did. Once more his insight proved right. Thinking back to Jo Wheelwright, to me, he was a grand father figure.

One more man must be given credit. As I pursued my academic career it became a prerequisite to earn, what is called a terminal degree, better known as a PhD. After a lengthy search and all possible postponements, I entered Golden Gate University in San Francisco.

On of my very first classes was conducted by the president of the university, Dr. Otto Butz. I forget the exact title of the course, but it covered the relationship of business and society. To my horror five thick books were  the required reading. After the very first class meeting I was convinced that I was on the right track, and that Dr. Butz surely was the brightest and most stimulating intellect I had ever met. For the first time in my life, learning was fun.

During the semester Dr. Butz encouraged us to start thinking about our dissertation, and as soon as the topic was approved, start working on it. I submitted my ideas to him, and not only did he approve, but suggested that he become the chair of my PhD committee. As we met periodically thereafter,  Otto was pleased with my progress and gave me free rein to lard my paper with my ideas and stay away from the typical dissertation content, which all too often is nothing more than a rearranging of prior work. "Your ideas are good, forget about what others have said. Stay original and forget about the usual blizzard of footnotes", were his encouraging instructions.

About half way through my program I submitted my first 200 odd pages for his review. The very next morning Otto was on the phone asking me to drop in, saying that we were "on the wrong track". I was demolished when he later told me that my work was not scholarly enough and that I needed to rework all I had done. Had I misunderstood him? Probably Otto realized that the first dissertations coming out of his new program had to fit the standard format. For two weeks I stopped all work and considered dropping out. Then I leaned back into the task and added about 200 footnotes to the work I had done and resubmitted my work. Otto was delighted with what was ostensibly the same content, only now supported by the "insight" of others.

As I finished my last two classes I concurrently submitted my dissertation to my committee. I passed in both theaters. What became most important to me was that Otto told me that my writing style was "brilliant" and that I had missed my métier. I should write for a living.

This father figure, a man I openly admired, gave me confidence that I could measure up intellectually. His friendship became a rock on which I hooked my anchor.

They all are gone now, yet will survive in me as long as I live.

These vignettes warrant some general conclusions.

A good father and son relationship must first and foremost be based on love and general approval offered by the parent. The result of this condition will be a feeling of being OK in the son, a foundation for self confidence and empowerment.

A father's role must include an introduction into masculinity. He should also provide basic values to live by. It is critically important for a father to offer assurance and reassurance in times of anxiety and uncertainty.

Much of life is a universal struggle and a father should equip his son with defenses, both rational and irrational. They, in turn, are ideally based on mutual trust. A father's supportive role should include the acceptance of authority by the son, this a validation of trust.

In our experience we have found all too often that sons are treated as mere extensions of the parent. Worse, many sons are treated as punching bags , a release for the father's frustrations and disappointments.

The FRASIER TV series provides an excellent example of father-son relations gone wrong. Martin Crane, the father of Frasier and Niles offers little but criticism and derision about his offspring. Their manhood is constantly questioned by Martin due to their lack of interest in sports and their preoccupation with esoteric arts and wine snobbery. The father, in this case, even questions their obvious success in their profession, psychiatry. Unforgettable is the show were Frasier is wheedling to try and get his father to say: "I love you!". After much prompting, "dad" finally does with little conviction.

### Lynda's Life and Times.

The second case covers Lynda's youth. An abandoned infant, an ignored child can be compared to a smashed clay pot. It will take many hours to attempt to glue it back together. And when done, fine lines, like scars will remain forever where the pieces meet.

I was born on July 29, 1931 in what was then called Peking, China. Right after seeing the light of my first day I was turned over to an Amah, a Chinese nanny, for care taking. There are several old faded photos of me with this woman, not one of me with my parents.

When I was three months old my mother and I, with another Chinese woman left China for my grandparent's ranch in California. War had broken out in Manchuria and our departure was seen as necessary to avoid getting caught in the conflict. My father, however, stayed in China where he was involved in the "Thousand Character Movement", an effort to teach 1000 characters to illiterate peasants. Together with the founder of the movement, Jimmy Yen, he traveled all over China and I did not see him again until I was 18 months old.

My Chinese caretaker left a few weeks after we got settled on the ranch. She objected to the verbal abuse my grandfather dished out to her just for being Chinese. I have no recall of who took care of me then, it was not my mother, perhaps a Mexican woman, the wife of one of the men who lived and worked on the ranch.

I was about 10 months old when my mother left to join her uncle Lincoln Steffens, my grandmother's brother in the Soviet Union. Steffens was an early supporter of the Russian revolution in 1917 and of Communism. My mother was fascinated by him and shared his idealism.

A few months later, I was perhaps 18 months old, I was uprooted again. My mother returned and together we moved to London to meet my father who had decided to attend medical school there to become a Jungian analyst. Since money was tight, we lived in a poor area in Chelsea with two rooms in the basement and two on the first floor.

My parents related two events which happened to me during this time. One happened soon after we arrived when a doctor checked my tonsils. He had one of those big mirrors on his forehead and after I exhaled on it, I shouted: "Jesus, it's steam", having already adopted the slang of my neighborhood.

The second story covers a vacation trip we took together by car to Brittany in France. I was about two and a half and screamed non stop all the way there. My father laughed about it later, telling his audience that I was as stiff as a board while crying in anger. I can only imagine that I feared that I was being moved again, no doubt about to lose my parents once more.

About this time, while in London, my mother became pregnant again. Later she acknowledged that she really had not wanted another child. I hunch she never wanted any child. It also occurs to me that my screaming on that ill fated trip to France was a reflection of her deep negative feelings about her pregnancy, feelings so intense that I picked them up.

My brother was born in November 1934 when I was three years, three months old. Six weeks later my mother fell into a post-partum psychosis which took the form of catatonia. She could do nothing by herself and had to be moved by others. She completely absorbed my father's attention while he was still attending medical school. To try and keep us together, both a nurse and a nanny were hired. The nanny was a nice woman from whom I learned and adopted a full bore Cockney accent, which outraged my father.

After some time my father took my mother to Zurich in the hope that Carl Jung would see and help her. Later I was told that Jung did not want to work with her since he already was fully booked with patients, with most of them being women. My father managed to pique Jung's interest by pointing out the split between the primitive and the civilized worlds in my mother's psyche. This was based on her upbringing on the cattle ranch far from any city and social life. This down to earth existence was followed by her being sent to sophisticated girls' schools in Santa Barbara and New York at the age of eight. Following that exposure she was sent to Bryn Mawr, a highly rated and demanding college. She escaped from there after one year to live with her uncle Steffens in Italy.

Jung was convinced and my mother claimed that after one visit with him, she came out of her psychosis. Yet it took many more months before she was able to even see my brother and me. She was completely remote when we finally saw her again and remained more or less so during my entire childhood.

When I turned six, my brother three, we moved from London to Zurich where my parents wished to continue their analyses with Jung and planned to start their own training as psychoanalysts. I recall getting along all right, going to school and learning Swiss German. I even made some friends. My brother John, however, began to deteriorate, feeling persecuted by the local kids because he could not understand or speak their language. As a last resort my parents sent us both back to England to an establishment for disturbed children in the small village of Withyham, Sussex. Many years later my mother admitted to me that "we sacrificed you so that you could be John's companion."

My recall of the place is scant. The two sisters who ran it were nice ladies. Their dog Judy became my friend and we walked together through chestnut forests and fields of blooming bluebells which still sticks in my mind. But there was a big bald boy who terrorized us little kids. We did not complain about him, we did not dare to.

We lived in this establishment for two years. My parents told me that they came for two visits which I do not remember. "You seemed ok and did not cry when we left", they told me later. I can only guess that I did not cry because I would have been laughed at for crying.

World War II was looming. I must have overheard the conversation of the adults and was aware of the threat of planes which might drop bombs. As a result, whenever I heard a plane at night, I dove under the bed, totally terrified. There was no one in whom I could confide my fears or seek help. Finally in the spring of 1939, a few months before the war broke out, my parents came to fetch us. Our mother then brought us back to the US on the SS Washington, a boat trip I recall as having been great fun. From New York we flew to Los Angeles on a DC3 with a sleeper setup. The flight, which took 12 hours and included several refueling stops, is a vivid memory.

In Los Angeles we were picked up and driven to the family ranch. There a new life waited for me. I had to relate to and deal with my wild cousins who were horse and cattle oriented. Adapting to their way of speaking, away from my metropolitan life and English accent was hard indeed. My getting to know their way of life, living in the wilderness, all left a permanent impact about which I wrote later in my book *The Long Shore*.

My brother and I lived on the ranch for two years while my parents got settled in San Francisco where my father did his internship at SF General. They lived in a tiny apartment in the Mission district and I was told that they could not afford to have us stay with them.

On the ranch, grandmother did not like children any better than my parents did. As a result another nanny was hired. She was, to us an ancient English lady whom we were told to call Miss Annis. She spent most of her time taking care of John who turned sickly with an assortment of respiratory troubles. Grandmother lived in another part of the house which was off limits to us. We rarely saw her or grandfather.

In 1941, at last, our parents called us home, to their new house in Marin County, north of San Francisco. Another nanny was put in charge of us. She was Mrs. McGinnis, to us a monster. She beat her daughter, who shared her bedroom, night after night. One day she got mad at John and with a large knife in her hand, approached my brother. She then whacked it across the back of his chair, breaking the blade in two, with one part flying across the room. We both were stiff with fright and worked hard not to antagonize her ever again. Not one word was said to our parents. We had no base of support.

Eventually this horror woman left and Miss Annis returned to help us all. My life took on some sort of normalcy. A daily routine consisted of my brother and me getting up for breakfast with Miss Annis, after which we left for school. Our parents rose after we had left and both went to work in San Francisco. They returned after John and I had gone to our rooms in the evening. On Saturdays my father got up around noon to do carpentry and other chores around the house, or see patients. My mother did household chores and also saw patients. On Sundays we all would go sailing in my father's sailboat. A day sail was all we could stand being so close together. My memories of these days focus on John being seasick, my father looking harassed and anxious. My mother was silent, as usual. I spent as much time as possible alone in the bow of the boat.

When I was 15 my father's brother George bought several hundred acres in the valley reaching down to Muir Beach, a few miles north of San Francisco. He turned this land into a cattle ranch, called Green Gulch Ranch, and allowed me to keep a horse of my own together with his herd of about a dozen stable horses. Since I was an experienced rider by now, I was given the job of taking groups of eight to ten year old children out on rides on weekends. I would pick them up at a bus station, about half an hour away and drive them to the ranch. I was asked to perform the same task and drive a car pool of school mates from their houses to school. Only years later did I feel a shock when I recognized the responsibility which had been piled on me on the assumption that I would take care of others and did not require being taken care of myself.

Also when still 15 I was assigned my first official "patient". She was a couple of years younger than I and I took her out on Saturday mornings for a ride. "Just keep her talking" were the instructions from my parents. "You don't have to do anything but teach her how to ride and listen to her" completed my duty list.

For two years we went out most Saturdays and she talked and talked. When I went off to college, we corresponded for some years, even after she got married. Gradually the letters stopped. She had found her own life. This experience profoundly affected me, and had much to do with my eventual capitulation into becoming a Jungian analyst, just like my parents.

I was still in my mid teens when I fell into a serious depression. It eased a bit when I started college studies at Cal, but remained with me for another 30 years. A harrowing trek through the Himalayas broke this ongoing pain. It took a personal crisis in my early 30's to start my own analysis. My analyst heard little from me other than constant sobbing.

Looking back from the present, I paid my dues with painful auto-immune disorders. It all began with temporal arteritis with concurrent fibromyalgia. It took three years to defeat the former and the fibromyalgia is now manageable.

Grief and sorrow were the causes of my distress. Crying was a release, but to me there is a level of grief, so deeply rooted that it cannot be reached. It may well stay with me forever. When I was very young I learned to repress my unpopular feelings, especially sadness. The total lack of relationship I had with my mother, even before my brother was born, was a permanent wound. This goes back to being a baby when I had no language, thus I may be unable to ever reach the despair of those early days. They found expression in my psychosomatic symptoms.

Added to my own sadness was what I absorbed from others. Going back to my first "patient", I realize that I have tended to relate to others from the stance of therapist. I kept my own stories buried and took on theirs. Now I have been a therapist officially for about 40 years, but in fact have been on duty for 60. No doubt some of the grief I carry is not my own, but that of others I carry with me.

A few years ago I had a dream in which Klaus and I are standing on a steep side hill, on a narrow path, looking down on a horrendous river roiling and churning below us. It was the sort of scene we lived through in the Himalayas, where the rivers were so fierce that you would have been ground to bits by the rolling boulders, had you fallen in. In the dream I see five or six elephants moving toward the river. They proceed to build a series of dams, pushing huge rocks into place across the river with their heads. With their trunks, they picked up smaller rocks with which they filled holes in the dam. One elephant pulled a rock out from under where we were standing, and we had to hustle along to a safe place on the path. I marveled at the work they were doing but could not see how it would benefit us. As I continued to watch them, the flow of water over the dam and down the river actually began to slow.

To me, elephants are wonderful, protective, loving mothers. It is my dream and the roaring waters are part of my grief. Yet the elephants were not relating to us and the one which pulled the rock out from under us was not trying to hurt us. I think they were working on collective sadness and pain, the grief of the world.

My dream, my psyche is sending me a message to differentiate my own grief from that of others, from that of the world. I am responsible for my own misery and for working on it, for resolving it. But I must separate the pain of others from my own and quit trying to carry the world on my back. My call to myself....Lighten up, carry only what you can, help those you can, drop the rest. Leave it to the "Big Something Up There".

## About the Authors

Lynda W. Schmidt is a Jungian Psychoanalyst and a member of the San Francisco Jung Institute. Her academic credentials were earned at the University of California, Berkeley. She has been in practice for nearly 40 years and is a training analyst. Most of her clients are fellow professionals. Lynda has written a number of books relating her psychological insight to nature and her California life.

Klaus D. Schmidt received his academic degrees from UC Berkeley, Stanford and Golden Gate University. His interests in analytical psychology were kindled by his foster mother, Mary Briner, a prominent analyst in Zurich Switzerland. Later, Joseph B. Wheelwright, who became his father in law, instilled a permanent search for insight in Klaus. Klaus authored a series of booklets for Stanford Research Institute in the socio cultural area.

www.ingramcontent.com/pod-product-compliance
Lightning Source LLC
Chambersburg PA
CBHW051420280526
45785CB00003B/1093